BRASS CASTLES

WEST YORKSHIRE NEW RICH
AND THEIR HOUSES 1800-1914

BRASS CASTLES

WEST YORKSHIRE NEW RICH
AND THEIR HOUSES 1800-1914

GEORGE SHEERAN

TEMPUS

For Tom, Chris and Emily

First published by Ryburn Pyblishing Ltd 1993,
new edition by Tempus Publishing Ltd 2006

Tempus Publishing Limited
The Mill, Brimscombe Port,
Stroud, Gloucestershire, GL5 2QG
www.tempus-publishing.com

British Library Cataloguing in Publication Data.
A catalogue record for this book is available from the British Library.

ISBN 0 7524 3806 9

Typesetting and origination by Tempus Publishing Limited
Printed in Great Britain

CONTENTS

ACKNOWLEDGEMENTS

The largest part of my thanks should go to the owners or occupiers of the many houses that I recorded. Without their co-operation this book would not have come to be written. Some people deserve special thanks for their continuing help and patience. They are Messrs Baileys of Ilkley, Mr and Mrs Clark of Malsis School, Mr Ken Pinder of Whinburn Schools Support Centre, Mrs Warrington of Bradford Girls' Grammar School, Mrs Whewell of Leeds University and Mr Woolnough of Moorlands School.

Documentary research left me indebted to another group of people and they are the staffs of West Yorkshire Archive Service, the Brotherton Library and Kirklees and Bradford Libraries. I should like to thank the staff at WYAS Headquarters, in particular, both for allowing me unrestricted access to probate calendars and for their help generally. I should like to add that they were a pleasure to work with and made me feel thoroughly at home. Similarly, I should like to thank Gordon Burton at the Map Bank of Wakefield Council who went to some considerable trouble to locate plans for me. Some documents remain in private hands, and I should like to thank a number of individuals and organisations for making their collections available to me: Alison Armstrong of Cliffe Castle, Patrick Boreham, Mr and Mrs Harrison, Caroline Mejloumian, Tim Morrell and Irene Orchard, as well as Jacques Chapotot of the Nuffield Institute, University of Leeds, and Neil Foster and Graham Creswick of John Foster & Son.

Other people supplied expert knowledge or comment. Among the former I should like to thank John Goodchild, Nigel Herring, Edward Law and also Colin Stansfield. For comment on the text I am indebted to my wife, Yanina, to David Baldwin of Manchester University, to Colum Giles of RCHM and to the late Dr David James. This book would have been the poorer without their suggestions.

Since I wrote the above acknowledgements to the first edition of this book other people have written to me to add further comments, supply further information and, dare I say it, to point out one or two errors. I should like to record my continuing thanks to A.W.R. Brook, Jean K. Brown, David Cant and Tony Heginbottom.

Photographic Acknowledgements

Patrick Boreham – *Hayfield House; Sutton Hall.* Bradford Art Galleries and Museums – *Strong Close House; servants at Eastwood House; Oakworth House; Cliffe Castle/Billiard Room/Music Room.* Calderdale Leisure Services (Museums and Arts) – *Bankfield.* Neil Foster – *Littlemoor/Drawing Room/Morning Room/Conservatory.* Kirklees Cultural Services – *Dining Room and Study, Rein Wood.* Caroline Mejloumian – *Longwood Hall.* Tim Morrell – *Bowling Park and carriage.* Nuffield Institute, Leeds – *Woodsley House/Drawing Room.* Royal Commission on the Historical Monuments of England – *Mill House, Barkerend, Bradford; Broadfold House, Luddenden.* Shipley Local History Society – *Billiard Room and Hall at Milnerfield.* WYAS, Kirklees – *Kirk & Sons' Plan of Rein Wood.* WYAS, Leeds – *Boudoir and Bathroom at Gledhow Hall.*

Abbreviations

BCL   Bradford Central Library
[D]   demolished
PP   Parliamentry Papers
WYAS   West Yorkshire Archive Service

7

INTRODUCTION

Fifty years have changed the appearance of everything in Rooms Lane ... From the knoll, near Benjamin Ward's farm, we have now lost the ancient farmer who ruled over the solitude, and in his place we have one of a race of self-made nobles – born of trade and commerce – whose pretty villa as it crowns the hill top is no disadvantage to the landscape ... Adorning the opposite hill ... is the large and ornate mansion of another of these nobles.[1]

This is a comment on the country around Morley, near Leeds, made in 1886 by William Smith, a local historian. The exact location does not matter: drive anywhere in West Yorkshire and you will find the same thing – handsome nineteenth-century mansions, some hidden away down private drives, others occupying commanding sites on valley sides with industry and towns down below. Few may be single private residences now, and the majority may have been turned into hotels or nursing homes or converted into apartments, yet they are as much a part of the Yorkshire scene as Dales farms, mill chimneys or pie and peas. Remarkably though, they have been paid little serious attention, and have never been explored as a group in their own right. In order to set the record straight, I began this study, a study of houses built by some of the wealthiest families in nineteenth-century West Yorkshire. Before I go any further, a word or two about the methods used is in order.

The first question that arises is what constitutes wealth? I have adopted the criterion used by some historians, notably by W.D. Rubinstein[2], of a minimum gross probate value of £100,000. The nineteenth-century middle class – and the study deals exclusively with them – can then be structured into the following wealth groups:

Those leaving estates worth:

£5,000-£25,000	the affluent
£25,000-£99,000	lesser wealth
£100,000-£499,000	superior wealth
£500,000-£999,000	half-millionaires
£1,000,000+	millionaires

It is mainly the last three groups with which I am concerned.

However, unlike Rubinstein, I have not made probate valuations the sole criterion, since they are not the cold and objective index to wealth that he and some other authors take them to be. Entrepreneurs such as Benjamin Gott and John Marshall of Leeds, for example, were judged millionaires by contemporaries, and their incomes, the sorts of houses they built or acquired, the art collections they amassed, as well as the huge industrial concerns they created suggest that contemporaries were correct in their assessments. Yet their probate valuations place them only among the superior wealth group. Here, gifts made during life can sometimes distort the image of a person's wealth. Thus, Sir Isaac Holden of Oakworth House was reputed to be the wealthiest man in the House of Commons when he took his seat as Liberal MP for Keighley in the 1880s. After his death in 1897 his estate was valued at £317,635, a value that belied his true worth – he had made gifts of £2 million to his children before his death.[3]

Another problem with probate figures is that they give us only a snapshot of wealth at the time of death. During his lifetime a person may have been worth a great deal more. There were, for example, some spectacular bankruptcies in the nineteenth century, bankruptcies that carried men such as William Hirst – toasted by contemporaries as the father of the Yorkshire woollen industry – from the pinnacle of wealth to imprisonment for debt: Hirst had been ruined in the banking panic of 1825. And there are other anomalies. Edward Akroyd was joint heir to a vast fortune left by his father, Jonathan Akroyd of Halifax. When Edward died, he left an estate of only £1,200, but he also left two model villages, two churches and an immense Italianate villa; he had contributed liberally to charities and lavished sums of money on political campaigns, thus whittling away his share of the £300,000 estate his father had built up. It would be ludicrous to say that Edward Akroyd was not a wealthy man, but probate figures alone suggest he was not.

Obviously, other factors have to be taken into account. Family archives of personal papers help to flesh-out the figures, and there are other, obvious signs of wealth – the purchase of houses and land in other parts of the country, the expense of acquiring and running a house in London, charitable donations on a grand scale, model village and other building schemes or embarking on a political career, a process which, if it culminated in a seat in the House and an active life in politics, could prove costly. Another factor to be taken into account, especially in this study, is house size. A house of any pretensions was not only expensive to build, but had to be furnished, decorated, staffed and maintained before the owner might even think about such things as entertaining. John Beaumont of Huddersfield, for example, spent around £20,000 on the construction of his house between 1859 and 1862; John Marshall of Leeds spent £3,000 a year in running his household at New Grange, Kirkstall – a sum well in excess of the annual incomes of the majority of the middle class. Thus, while probate valuations were my basic guide to wealth, they have been augmented where possible.

Another question arises as to how I chose the families to be studied. Using probate valuations it would have been possible to have compiled a list of all the people in the county leaving estates of above £100,000, but I did not pursue this course. To begin with, I was interested only in wealth newly created in the nineteenth century, and created from industrial, professional, commercial or financial endeavour. Because of this I excluded all landed families, that is, the old nobility and gentry of the county. I also excluded descendants of the commercial and financial nabobs of the eighteenth century. The Denisons and Becketts of Leeds may have been extremely wealthy families in nineteenth-century West Yorkshire, but they could hardly be considered newly rich, having ancestors from among the elite of Leeds commercial society well before 1800.

The families that do end up on my list, therefore, represent those who had grown rich during the Industrial Revolution. Even so, the list is selective. If the list of families were to be of any use, then reasonably good biographies concerning marriage, kinship, social origins and business career had to be available, and for some they were not. Then there were

9

problems of chronology. While those people born before about 1860 might reasonably be supposed to have made their fortunes during the remainder of the century, things are not so clear-cut when it comes to people born after that date, especially if they lived to a great age. The Taylor family of Batley are a case in point. As woollen manufacturers they were a successful firm, but individual members of the family never showed signs of great wealth. Theodore Cooke Taylor was born in 1850; when he died, he had lifted the family fortunes into the superior wealth category, leaving £185,233 – but that was in 1952 at the age of 102; moreover, much of this fortune had probably been made during the First World War and the boom years that followed. Similarly, Ernest H. Gates, born in 1873, grew to a man of some importance in Bradford, eventually becoming a director of Saltaire Mills and leaving nearly £1 million when he died in 1925. Again, much of this fortune was made after the First World War. But there were others who made their fortunes in a few years towards the end of the century – Sir Joshua Kelly Waddilove, for example. Although born in 1841, he did not form his own business until 1880, but progress and profits were so rapid that he was able to retire in 1905. He died in 1920 leaving an estate worth £1,260,000 after making substantial contributions to charities. Obviously, the business careers of those born after the middle of the century needed careful examination to determine whether they were nineteenth- or twentieth-century new rich.

A fundamental requirement for inclusion on my list concerned houses. If a family were to be chosen, then the houses they built, or houses associated with them, had to survive. If a house had been demolished, then good photographic or documentary evidence had to exist.

In this way ninety-two families and details of nearly 200 individuals, were chosen. Incomplete data on many more families then provided a useful reserve of ancillary information. I decided that family groupings rather than individuals were more relevant to the task in hand, provided that at least one member of the family came into the category of superior wealth or above. Thus, a family's housing developments in relation to wealth could be examined, and so could groupings of family houses in a particular area. The nature of many nineteenth-century manufacturing and commercial concerns really necessitates a study of families rather than focusing on an individual, especially with regard to wealth. As one historian has observed:

> The pattern of industry itself made wealth more familial than personal. The capital requirements of high-profit production meant that a firm's assets could not be divided up every generation.[4]

On the other hand, as Rubinstein has noted[5], it was unusual for a large personal fortune to be handed on intact to one individual member of a family; it would usually be parcelled out into smaller sums and distributed amongst various members. This was one reason why heirs of millionaire fathers did not become billionaires in the course of time. Such points of view are complementary, and the transmission of business, houses and wealth or the drift away from business to investment in land and a country estate are an essential part of this study.

Although I feel that this more sociological approach to architectural history is fully justified, the principal concern is architecture, nevertheless. It is in some ways surprising that, even today, few serious studies of Victorian middle-class houses have been produced. There was, indeed, what amounted to a hatred of Victorian architecture until the post-war years, and it was not until the last quarter of the twentieth century that an appreciation of the quality of much Victorian work appeared in print. Even so, there remains a reluctance to protect some Victorian houses, and there are no official histories of the middle-class house in the region – no inventories or publications by the former Royal Commission on Historical Monuments, for example. Where books have appeared, there are weaknesses even in the best of authors: skimpy national surveys that tend to over-represent well-known houses – Cragside, for instance – or the lumping together of all large houses as 'country houses'. Only Derek Linstrum in his work on Yorkshire architecture[6] has recognised and tried to define the differences between the country house on the one hand, and the houses of some wealthy manufacturers on the other, coining the term 'villa mansions' to describe the latter. Unfortunately, Linstrum left matters there.

If we are to gain a fuller understanding, then we must go further: we need to identify houses with their wealthy owners, ask questions about their money and how they made it; about their social origins and aspirations; about how they regarded their social position and their houses. In short, we must enter the world of Victorian wealth.

CHAPTER ONE
THE NEW RICH DEFINED

The Pattern of Wealth

In 1795, Edward Lascelles was fifty-three years old and heir to a great fortune left to him by his cousin Lord Harewood. Although by no means the poor relation of the family, he was considerably enriched by his inheritance: he now owned Harewood House together with its furniture and art collection, a collection that he was to further enhance. His income arising from land was above £20,000 a year, and this was supplemented by income from the family estates in the West Indies. In 1808 his total income was assessed at £46,284, and we can add to all this the cash fortune of around £200,000 that he had also inherited.[1]

Lascelles, or the Earl of Harewood as he later became, was among the richest men in the county. For generations such families had derived their livings from lands they held in West Yorkshire and elsewhere. They were great farmers in their own right and the recipients of agricultural rents from their tenants; they were also industrialists, deriving further profits from coal, ironstone or other mineral deposits that lay under their land. The grandest of these families lived in the east of the modern county, mostly between Leeds and Wakefield, where farming land and communications were better – the Meynall-Ingrams of Temple Newsam, the Earl of Mexborough at Methley Hall, the Lowthers at Swillington House, the Blands at Kippax Park and the Beaumonts (later the Lords Allendale) at Bretton Hall. Their incomes ranged from Thomas Davison Bland's £10,126 a year to Mrs Meynall-Ingrams's £45,491. While the estates of some families were trusts in which they had a life interest only, others built up huge personal fortunes – when W.B. Beaumont, 1st Baron Allendale, died in 1901, he left an estate worth £3,189,000.

There were also other, less wealthy gentlemen living on modest estates in other parts where they too might have been settled for many generations. Generally speaking their incomes were derived from the same sources as their wealthier neighbours, but were smaller, usually in the range of £4,000-£10,000 a year. A good example is William Busfeild-Ferrand of St Ives, Harden. Born William Busfeild, a descendant of a gentle family living in the Bingley district, he was eventually to inherit the Bingley estates of the Ferrand family, another gentle family, to whom the Busfeilds were related by marriage. He rebuilt the old family home and landscaped the grounds; he had decided political views, became an MP, a friend of Disraeli and Lord John Manners, and as a justice was feared and respected in the district. In 1879, his landed income[2] stood at £7,698. Families like these represented traditional wealth, old money, that went back as far as the seventeenth century in some cases, and landed families remained a major wealth-holding group throughout the nineteenth century. They were a group, moreover, that few could compete with in terms of wealth, and none in terms of pedigree.

To gain some idea of just how very wealthy these people were it is interesting to compare their incomes with wage levels in the manufacturing districts of the county. There are several sources we might go to for information of this sort, but one of the most useful is the inquiry initiated by the Bradford merchant Sir Jacob Behrens[3] into the condition of the working class of Bradford and the surrounding districts in the 1880s. One of the things that the inquiry reported on was wage levels between 1875 and 1885, which were thought, generally, to be improving. The best paid were workers in the iron, steel and engineering industries – boilermakers, for example, were amongst the most highly paid at 38 shillings a week. At the other end of the scale the most lowly paid were shop assistants, men and women being paid 15 shillings and 13/6d respectively for a seventy-hour week, although this sum included the provision of meals. The majority of the working population were employed in the textile industry. Here, the best wages averaged 28 shillings to 30 shillings a week for overlookers, sinking to the 12-shilling wage of female carders for a fifty-six-and-a-half-hour week. Of course, a couple of children at work might boost family income by 15 shillings to £1. Thus, the combined family income of a skilled man whose wife remained at home, but with two children at work, might be £2-£3 a week, £100-£150 a year. A single unskilled man, on the other hand, might earn as little as £30-£40 a year. Compared with the income of even a middling gentleman at, say, £5,000 a year, the gulf is enormous.

The gulf was not so great, however, between the best working-class incomes and the majority of middle-class incomes. Over the years, historians have made differing estimates of middle-class incomes – some have defined the lower limit at as little as £50; others[4] have suggested an average of around £300. More accurate assessments can be found in Parliamentary Papers. In the 1860 session of Parliament, for example, taxation returns were published showing the numbers of people paying tax in 1858 under schedule D – profits arising from trade, industry or a profession, and, thus, most of the middle class.[5] For taxation purposes, income was divided into eighteen bands from under £100 a year to above £50,000 a year. The largest group of taxpayers had incomes of £100-£150 yearly which was the average income also. The number of taxpayers reduced rapidly after the £400-£500 band was passed, and only 9,874 people or 3.7% of taxpayers earned above £1,000 a year. This is a national figure. As a percentage of those paying schedule D this is small; as a percentage of the wage-earning population it would be microscopic. The above also agrees with the findings of other commentators. Jack Reynolds[6], for instance, found that a similar return of 1880 relating to Leeds, Bradford, Huddersfield and Manchester, showed that just over a third of taxpayers in these places earned between £100 and £150. W.D. Rubinstein[7] quotes figures relating to the income tax of 1801 showing that the majority of those taxed earned between £60 and £150.

The conclusion to be drawn from figures such as these is that we should revise our opinions of middle class wealth in the nineteenth century. The majority of the middle class had modest incomes not far above the incomes of better-off working-class families. While there were, nevertheless, a fair number of middle-class families earning above £200 a year, few earned above £1,000, and it is this minority, composed of highly paid professionals, merchants, commercial and industrial magnates, that the rest of this chapter is concerned with.

The Magnates

By the nineteenth century, the area that we today call West Yorkshire had become the premier wool textile-producing region of the country. Leeds was its commercial and industrial capital, but by the mid-nineteenth century its pre-eminence was challenged by Bradford, a place that had been little more than a market town in the preceding centuries, yet displaced Leeds as the mercantile centre of the county and became the international centre of the worsted industry, also. The position of Leeds and Bradford was reflected both in the sizes of their populations and industrial profitability which far exceeded the other West Yorkshire boroughs – Dewsbury, Halifax, Huddersfield and Wakefield.[8] It is no surprise, therefore, that larger numbers of fortunes were made in these places, and that the greatest numbers of fortunes were made by textile entrepreneurs.

What is surprising is the relative smallness of many textile fortunes. This was the result, perhaps, of textiles being a high turnover, low profit margin industry: in other words, you had to work very hard to put away above £100,000 by the end of your life. The Talbot family of Batley and their partner Samuel Senior are typical of many woollen manufacturers. They had mills in both Batley and Morley, and had done a brisk trade supplying the armies of Europe with blankets and cloth for uniforms, a trade boosted by the emergence of Prussian militarism. On the profits of trade they had all established small estates and good houses within a stone's throw of one another at Upper Batley; when they died, they were worth £40-£50,000 apiece. This sort of money is what one might expect of the majority of successful textile manufacturers in nineteenth-century West Yorkshire. This is not to say that superior wealth did not exist. Across the valley from the Talbots at Batley Carr lived Mark Oldroyd, another woollen manufacturer, who left £93,100 when he died. In Leeds, Robert Hudson and William Ledgard had amassed fortunes of £100,000, and the same can be found in some of the towns around Leeds. Hard work and a modest lifestyle probably account for the £295,500 left by William Murgatroyd of Moorfield Mills, Yeadon, and George Webster of Gildersome can similarly be placed in the superior wealth group. The Mitchells, Garnetts and Illingworths were all Bradford worsted families leaving between £100,000 and £300,000, and similar worsted men could be found in Calderdale, Airedale and the Worth Valley – the Murgatroyds of Luddenden or the Merralls of Haworth, for instance. Wakefield should not be excluded from the picture. The major families here were the Marriotts and Barkers, worsted spinners, with estates at the £200-£300,000 level. To say that these fortunes were of superior wealth only is not to denigrate their significance. A family with £50,000, let alone £100,000, was considered rich in the nineteenth century, and greater sums were a rarity – the Registrar General's report[9] on the working of the new 1858 Probate Act, for example, shows that throughout the nation only sixty-seven wills were proved for estates of above £100,000 in that year.

But textiles, like any other industrial sector, had its super-rich. I have already mentioned Benjamin Gott of Leeds in this context. Another, though less well-known, woollen millionaire was Samuel Eyres of Armley who left an estate worth £1,200,000 in 1868. In Bradford, Isaac Holden was a millionaire wool comber, while Titus Salt was of at least half-millionaire status and had spent a further £250,000 in the construction of his model village, Saltaire. Other half-millionaires included John Beaumont of Huddersfield who made his money providing designs for that most Victorian article of clothing the fancy waistcoat. The reason why such businessmen prospered beyond their competitors was not simply superior business acumen – although this they seem to have had in good measure – but inventive genius or an eye for possibilities that others had not seen. Thus, Holden and his one-time partner, Lister, had been instrumental in the mechanisation of the wool

In some towns, sophisticated industrial buildings can be found. Temple Mills, Leeds, were erected for John Marshall between 1838 and 1843 to a design by Joseph Bonomi, and were to cost Marshall £52,474 for the buildings alone. What Marshall got for his money was a brilliant pastiche of the Ptolemaic temples of ancient Egypt.

combing process, Lister charging the handsome royalty of £1,000 on each of his machines; Salt had pioneered the use of alpaca yarns to produce mixed-fibre worsted cloths with a lustrous sheen, the very cloth that much of Bradford's nineteenth-century prosperity was based on; Beaumont had not only introduced fancy weaving into the worsted trade (it had been largely restricted to the woollen), but also designed new patterns, patterns to which he retained the copyright, and, presumably, the royalties due; Gott can be credited with introducing large-scale mechanised factory production into the woollen industry, while at the same time extending the mercantile branch of his firm.

Wool textiles was not the only textile industry. Flax was of great importance to Leeds in the first half the nineteenth century, and here John Marshall reigned supreme. More about his wealth follows. Cotton promoted other families to riches. The Fieldens of Todmorden were the outstanding family in this sphere. John Fielden jnr left nearly half a million when he died in 1893, while his father and brother had each left above a million. Perhaps the largest cotton fortune – indeed, one of the largest fortunes – was made by Edward Brook, cotton thread manufacturer of Meltham Mills who amassed property worth £2,181,000, although income from his country estate at Ecclefechan, Dumfries, added a little to this. John Marshall was probably his equal, although Marshall's exact wealth is difficult to quantify.

Marshall, in fact, illustrates another point: wealth generated in the textile industry might be used for investment in other industries. Railways were a particular favourite in the mid-nineteenth century, and Marshall had invested £100,000 by 1838. This makes the few thousand that other manufacturers had invested pale into insignificance. However, Joseph Holdsworth, the Wakefield dyer, had invested nearly £70,000 and the Bradford worsted spinner and wool stapler William Murgatroyd had committed £62,812 in the 1840s and was later to become a director of the Midland Railway. Others invested in the railways, mines and industries in the emerging economies of continents such as South America. Such foreign investment makes a true assessment of wealth difficult, unless family papers exist, since it would not be taken into account for probate purposes. Henry Isaac Butterfield of Cliffe Castle, Keighley, left an estate of £220,000 when he died, but this was well short of his true worth, since he had undisclosed sums tied up in real estate in North America and France. Perhaps the quirkiest investment was that made by the Irish-born H.C. McCrea of Halifax whose surplus profits from damask production were channelled into the development of the holiday resort of Blackpool and in particular the North Pier. He did well, leaving £294,000 at his death in 1901.

Dalton Mills, Keighley, were built in stages between about 1869 and 1877, for the worsted firm of J. & J. Craven. Although the influence is Classical, it is an eclectic classicism. The tops of towers, moreover, are like minarets, and originally the chimney (middle background) had a similar termination, thus strengthening the impression.

Factories of simpler design were more typical and might be found throughout the region, sometimes in Pennine locations such as Ebor Mill, Haworth. It represents a continuous development on the site from water to steam power between about 1819 and 1887. Rural concerns like this were, nevertheless, capable of generating huge profits.

The majority of factories, however, were built in the industrial towns where they polluted the environment appallingly. This print shows Bradford in the mid-nineteenth century.

There were several areas of production related to textiles – carpets, for example. Indeed, this sometimes emerged from a textiles background. The Firth family had been producing blankets in the Flush area of Heckmondwike for several generations, but during the course of the nineteenth century also went into carpet making, a venture that was to lead them to America where they established a factory in New York. Thomas Freeman Firth died in 1909 leaving an estate of £379,000. The outstanding name in carpets, however, was Crossley of Halifax. Their success was in harnessing the techniques of power loom weaving and volume production to the making of carpets. Eventually, their mills at Dean Clough grew to colossal proportions, filling the valley floor; their mansions formed a prominent feature in the south Halifax landscape; their Gothic almshouses and orphanage, their palazzo-style hotels and offices adorned the streets of Halifax, while as a family they made two or three fortunes in the magnitude of £500,000 to £1 million.

Machine making was another textile-related industry. Looms, jennies, roving, combing and carding machines all had their manufacturers. Keighley was the home of two prominent machine makers – R.L. Hattersley and Sir Prince Smith, the latter a millionaire. In Leeds, the Fairbairns became the biggest engineering employer. Peter Fairbairn had begun manufacturing machinery for the Leeds woollen and flax industry, but was later to diversify into machine tools for armament and locomotive manufacture. He was knighted by Queen Victoria for his services to the city, while his son Andrew, who became a partner in the firm, left a country house near York and £349,600 in 1901. The production of components was another thriving industry: cards and hackle pins, for example, were what T.R. Harding of Leeds made his money on, leaving an estate valued at £145,000 when he died in 1895. Other engineering products were of a more general application. Edward Green of Wakefield had invented 'Green's Fuel Economiser' which utilised waste flue gases to pre-heat water fed into boilers, thus saving costs on fuel. It was a great success and put the Greens on the road to becoming millionaires. Other engineers, inventors and patentees included George Bray of Leeds who put a new and improved gas burner on the market, a success story that took a man of originally modest means to an estate of above £232,000 by the end of the century.

The heavy engineering industry was also well represented. Outstanding was James Kitson, millionaire locomotive builder of the Airedale Foundry. Kitson also owned the Monkbridge Iron Works which his father had bought to provide a ready supply of iron. If iron and steel making did not take on the scale that they did in Sheffield or Middlesbrough, they were, nevertheless, of no small importance with several works scattered throughout the region. The really big concerns, however, were at Bradford – Bowling Iron Works and Low Moor Iron Works. J.G. Paley had been the driving force behind the Bowling Iron Works, while the Hardy and Dawson families controlled the vast undertakings at Low Moor where boiler plates, railway tyres, cannon for the armies of the Crimea and ordnance in general were cast. When a Quaker friend of Dawson, who had been a Presbyterian minister, was shown round the works, he was reported to have commented, 'Friend Joseph, has thy preaching come to this? Making things like these to kill thy fellow men?'[10] Friend Joseph and his son made above £250,000 at it, while their partners the Hardys became millionaires.

A reliable supply of pure chemicals was needed by several industries. High on the customer priority list in this area were the textile-related industries – scouring, dying, bleaching. They were sometimes supplied by well established, traditional firms such as the North Brook Chemical Works at Bradford that had been supplying vitriol for bleaching since the eighteenth century. The great increase in textile production in the nineteenth century boosted the Leather family, originally worsted spinners, but later proprietors of the chemical works, to much greater prosperity, indeed, to superior wealth. But as with other industries, innovation brought huge wealth, and the chemical works at Leeds and Wakefield of E.A. Brotherton are a good example. Brotherton had perfected a process for producing pure ammonia, a substance much sought after in both the woollen and the gold extraction industries – he died a millionaire.

Agriculture and the food and drink manufacturing industries are sectors where one might expect to find good profits in an increasingly populous and wealth-creating region. However, this was not so. Agricultural fortunes were scarce, indeed, almost non-existent in nineteenth-century West Yorkshire, for, as one commentator had observed of the Bradford district at the end of the eighteenth century, 'Land is possessed by small proprietors and occupied by small farmers and manufacturers ... the inhabitants having both their minds and capitals fixed upon trade.'[11] Most farms in the region, apart from the great gentry farms, were indeed small when compared with more fertile areas of the country. Those who remained in farming or those who began a new farm on recently enclosed moorlands, were engaged mostly in supplying the rising populations of the industrial towns with dairy products, but no one farmer seems to have introduced modern methods of marketing. It was a piecemeal operation involving hundreds of independent small farms, most of them making a living, but no-one getting rich. It was among the factors and merchants that money was to be made, men such as the Leeds corn merchant Thomas England who was to build himself the stately pile of Headingley Castle as his retreat from business. Similarly, food manufacturing produced no big-money names. The nearest the region came to this was in the person of Sir William Pickles Hartley, the jam king, but his business was situated at Colne, alas, just across the border in Lancashire. Brewing was a different question. Perhaps one firm more than any other became a household name in this part of Yorkshire – Joshua Tetley & Son, the Leeds-based brewery, whose later partners ranged from superior wealth to half-millionaires. But the wealthiest of the Yorkshire brewers was the bachelor Robert Arthington of Hunslet who was worth £1 million when he died in 1900, leaving £500,000 to the Baptist Missionary Society and £400,000 to the London Missionary Society.

Retailing, too, fares badly compared with most of the other industrial or commercial sectors. West Yorkshire did not have its Sainsbury, Lipton or W.H. Smith, nor the chain store moguls. With few exceptions, lesser wealth seems to have been the best that West Yorkshire shopkeepers could hope for. John Limber Morley of Bradford, for example, despite a string of pawn shops from Bradford to Cambridge, left only £35,000. Others began trading too late in the century to include in the study. Michael Marks did not set out his now legendary stall on Leeds market until 1884, and it was not until after the First World War that the fat profits came rolling into Marks & Spencer. Antonio Fattorini and his family had settled in Bradford in the mid-nineteenth century setting up a jewellery business and laying the foundations of their wealth selling accurate watches in a time-conscious age. But it was not until the end of the century that they opened the mail order operation that was eventually to become the big earner – Empire Stores.

Nor were there many great fortunes among the professions dominated by the middle class – solicitors, accountants, general practitioners, architects – as opposed to the old, gentry-dominated professions. Architects might be thought a particular interest of *this* study. They are, but no local architect appears to have accumulated an estate of more than lesser wealth. Thomas Campbell Hope of Bradford seems typical of many. Over a long working life he had designed many streets, individual houses and public buildings, mostly in Bradford, and, in common with other members of his profession, he had speculated in land and housing development in parts of the town. When he died in 1916 he left a comfortable house in Ilkley and an estate of £10,700. The wealthiest architects appear to have been Thomas Ambler of Leeds and Eli Milnes of Bradford leaving estates worth £45,000 and £31,000 respectively. One or two professional estates are worth mentioning, however. W.H. Armitage of Banney Royd, Huddersfield, for example, was an accountant who left his son an estate of £112,700; and the stockbroker F.W. Bentley, also of Huddersfield, left an estate worth £174,800.

The mention of stockbroking brings us to finance. Rubinstein's study of British wealth has shown that the greatest fortunes were made in commerce and finance, and that the largest number of those were located in London. It is interesting to compare West Yorkshire with this, where much wealth was based on manufacturing industry. If there was a thriving banking and commercial sector, many of the houses transacting the business were run by the old rich, the descendants of eighteenth-century firms and families, especially around Leeds. There were some new families, but, contrary to Rubinstein's findings, it is more common to find these new banking families and the fortunes they made located in the superior wealth category rather than anything greater. The Harris family of Bradford banking circles and the Tews of Pontefract are typical, leaving fortunes in the order of £100,000 to £300,000. The exception here were the Oxleys of Leeds, Henry Oxley leaving nearly £500,000, while his son, who became senior partner in the Leeds bank William Williams Brown, left one of the largest fortunes in the county at £2,686,000. Along with this we might rank the fortunes made in the new sorts of financial services that began to develop in the later nineteenth century, credit advance, for example. Such agencies would advance loans to their clients – mostly from the lower middle and working class – for the purchase of goods and clothing. Prolific, here, was the Provident Clothing and Supply Company, founded by Joshua Kelly Waddilove in Bradford in 1880. By the beginning of the twentieth century, the company employed 5,000 people, and Waddilove was able to retire a millionaire.

This chapter began with my comments on the sorts of incomes we might have expected to find in the county among the landowning, middle and working class. Although the magnates that I have been writing about certainly left great sums of money, equities or valuable art collections, details of their incomes are sketchy. The details that do exist suggest that incomes were usually well above £1,000 a year, and that they ranged from fabulous wealth to prosperous shares in company profits. For example, in the first half of the nineteenth century, John Marshall's earnings from his flax mills fluctuated between about £14,000 and £65,000 a year, while his contemporary Benjamin Gott was withdrawing as much as £120,000 a year by the 1830s as his share of the company profits.[12] Both men were reckoned to be millionaires when they died, and, indeed, this sort of income was a necessary requirement of millionaire status. In 1873, Joseph Henry Craven, a worsted spinner of Strong Close, Keighley, suffered a mental breakdown and was eventually committed. The Commissioners in Lunacy[13] assessed his income at £10,256, and his estate at £132,414. Joshua Tetley, the Leeds brewer, calculated that his income in 1841 amounted to nearly £3,000; he died in 1859 leaving an estate valued at £50,000.

Tetley illustrates another point, and that is the comparatively small value of the estates left by some entrepreneurs who died before 1870, particularly if they were the founders of firms. Usually, they come under the category of lesser wealth, while second and third generations might progress to superior wealth or above. There are perhaps several reasons for this, some varying from industry to industry, from family to family, but a common one was the need on the parts of founders of firms to re-invest profits in order to establish the business in its early days, especially where the founder had little capital to start with. This brings us to the question of social origins, and it is worth spending a little time on the subject, since it will reveal much about the lifestyles and attitudes to house-building of certain families.

Origins

In order to assess the social origins of newly rich families, I decided to look at the family backgrounds and paternal occupations of the founders of businesses. I was able to find such information for all of the families that I had been studying, and, in theory, it ought to have been possible to place them and preceding generations in one class or another. In practice things were not so simple. While landowning families, the old nobility and gentry, survived pretty much intact as a social group in the nineteenth century, the problems begin lower down the social scale, problems that arise when dealing with a society in the throes of change. The terms middle class and working class should not really be used to describe eighteenth-century ancestors, while the social rankings of the eighteenth century are of less and less significance in describing those born in the nineteenth century. In order to overcome this difficulty, I decided to make the following distinctions based on the origin of income:

Group 1	Those whose income or the greater part of it derived from land ownership (for instance the nobility and gentry).
Group 2	Those whose income derived from salaries, fees or the profits of trade or agriculture (for instance, professionals, merchants, master manufacturers, farmers).
Group 3	Wage earners employed in skilled or unskilled labour (for instance, outworkers in the textile industry, farm hands).

In this way, I hope, comparisons can be made between the centuries with better accuracy.

The results are rather interesting. To begin with, none of the newly rich families came from group 1. This is hardly surprising, since I had excluded nobility and gentry from the study, on the grounds that they represented old money. But it is still worth noting that although some newly rich group 2 families married with group 1 families, the latter were not the initiators of businesses. The Lister family of Bradford, for instance, have sometimes been thought of as gentlemen who went into trade, whereas it was the other way round: the worsted manufacturer Ellis Cunliffe married the niece of Samuel Lister, a landed gentleman of Manningham; later, Cunliffe inherited the Manningham estate through his wife's title and assumed the name Lister.

Very few families originated from group 3. Only six out of ninety-two had begun life as wage earners or had fathers who were wage earners. These were: Edward Baines who went from journeyman printer to proprietor of *The Leeds Mercury*; Isaac Holden, wool comber, son of a Scottish smallholder and coal miner, he himself starting his working life as a weaver's labourer; Ira and James Ickringill, worsted spinners, sons of a hand wool comber forced into factory employment following mechanisation – Ira and James had also been factory hands; Daniel and Miles Illingworth, worsted spinners, the sons of Phineas Illingworth, a farm labourer turned factory hand; James Kitson senior who began his working life in a dye works; William Shaw, railway contractor, who had been apprenticed to his father, a journeyman mason.

Newly rich families came overwhelmingly from group 2, those whose fathers and sometimes grandfathers had made their livings from the profits of trade or agriculture or the fees they had charged in the practice of a profession. This finding is in line with much modern thinking on the subject: that is, the rags to riches success stories so beloved of Victorian writers were in reality somewhat rare. In this respect, Samuel Smiles and his book *Self Help* published in 1859 are seen as the arch-villains, propagating the myth that through honesty, hard work and application, a man might rise, no matter what his circumstances. 'Practical industry, wisely and vigorously applied,' Smiles wrote, 'always produces its due effects ... All may not rise equally, yet each, on the whole, very much according to his desserts.'[14] This was the stuff of many a Victorian obituary or biography of a local worthy:

June 6th, 1845, Died, John Marshall Esq., at his seat Hallsteads, near Penrith, in the eightieth year of his age. The deceased was a native of Leeds, and is one of the most remarkable instances of men who have risen by their own talents, perseverance, and enterprise from moderate circumstances ... to the possession of a splendid fortune.

SEP 7th, 1855, Died aged 82, Joshua Bower Esq., at his residence Hillidge House, Hunslet ... Mr Bower was the architect of his own fortune, and succeeded in amassing a large fortune, and giving employment to hundreds of the inhabitants of Hunslet.[15]

Through their researches into the social origins of nineteenth-century entrepreneurs many present-day historians have come to view accounts such as the above with suspicion, and the whole idea of the self-made man with some scepticism. And yet, there is still much to be said for Smiles and others, once we have put their moralizing to one side. A careful examination of the backgrounds of group 2 families reveals that, despite their superior sources of income, the group was, nevertheless, dominated by small tradesmen and farmers who, if they were not poor, could in no way be considered rich. In other words, they were of humble origins. Granted, there was a wealthier element among them – Benjamin Gott's father might be thought of as a surveyor or civil engineer who was able to spend £400 in apprenticing his son to a Leeds merchant house; the father of John Hague, the

Dewsbury woollen manufacturer and banker, was a Dublin merchant who could provide his son with the money to set up a business in Yorkshire; Jeremiah Marshall was worth £10,000 when he died in 1787, and his second son, John, inherited his father's drapery shop which brought in £1,000 worth of business a year; Edward Allan Brotherton was the son of a Manchester cotton manufacturer who, with the help of family and friends, established his chemical manufacturing business.

But families like these were not typical. Within the textile industry it was more common for families to have been engaged in textile production for several generations, either as yeomen clothiers with small farms or as organisers of labour. While some owned the freehold of their land, and while their lifestyles were reasonably comfortable, nevertheless, they could not be counted among the wealthy of the county. Judging from surviving buildings and probate inventories, they lived mostly in vernacular houses, often farmhouses, well-furnished, but with an assortment of traditional and more up-to-date furniture. While they lacked none of life's comforts, they possessed few of its refinements. Occasionally, family diaries or other accounts turn up to confirm this view. The Taylor family, woollen manufacturers of Batley, were still living this kind of life in the 1850s in their house next to the mill, as recalled by Theodore Cooke Taylor:

> Many of us remember our former Blakeridge Offices, my grandfather's old home ... That house is described in the purchase deed as 'a dwelling house with shops over the same' ... The 'dwelling house', substantially stone built, faced south ... On the ground floor to the right was a fair sized room called 'the parlour', in which visitors were received. But against the back wall, and posing as a sideboard, was a large shut-up bedstead ... to the left from the front lobby, one entered the largest room, always called 'the house'. For one daughter, while she lived, and for the seven sons, none of whom married before the youngest was 21 ... it was dining room, talk room and reading room combined. In it was my grandfather's old-fashioned armchair, cushioned but made chiefly of round wooden rods.[16]

A kitchen and bedrooms occupied the rest of the ground floor. When John Shaw of Stainland died in 1820, his probate inventory reveals a parlour furnished with a corner cupboard, an oak table, two mahogany tables, six elm chairs and a press. This was the best room in the house – it hardly conveys a sense of wealth or luxury. John Shaw was the founder of the business and his estate was valued at £1,500, yet his family were to establish Brookroyd Mills, an important spinning concern; they progressed to lesser, then superior wealth; they became magistrates, deputy lieutenants of the county, and one became a Liberal MP.[17]

Of the ninety-two families examined, twenty-one could be said to have come from affluent families, the estates of the fathers of founders of businesses being between £1,000 and £10,000. The rest came from families lower down the wealth scale: at the bottom, as we have seen, were the wage-earning families, while the others left estates valued at between £200 and £1,000. Thus, although the majority of first-generation entrepreneurs may have begun their business careers with some capital, and often with a tradition of family endeavour in trade or leadership within the community, nevertheless, they came from humble origins. To jump from an estate worth, say, £800 to one worth above £100,000 within a generation was a very considerable leap. A number of textile families are typical in this respect. George Harrop of Osset had come from a long line of clothiers in a small way of business, and he himself had been a handloom weaver and organiser of labour. Not until 1858, when he was in his mid-forties, did he rent a room in a mill at Horbury and from there built his business into a highly profitable concern. He left an estate of over £121,000 when he died in 1892. Or take John Foster snr of Black Dyke

Mills. The son of a small farmer in the Thornton district of Bradford, he married Ruth Briggs in 1819, the daughter of another small farmer. Ruth could not even sign her name on the marriage certificate, but made a mark instead, while John has been described by E.M. Sigsworth as possessing 'only a rudimentary literacy'.[18] Yet Foster was to found a massive worsted concern at Black Dyke, Queensbury, managed by himself and his son William. When John died in 1878 he was worth £250,000, and William was to become a millionaire. As far as the wealthy individuals in this study are concerned, the phenomenon of the self-made man remains alive and well.[19]

A Silk Hat on a Bradford Millionaire

When T.S. Eliot used the above expression in *The Waste Land*, he was subscribing to a common misconception: the crude, untutored manufacturer, grown rich through industrial endeavour, and promoted, uneasily, beyond his station. In one respect this is nothing more than an age-old piece of snobbishness that sneers at new money. In another, it is the idea of quick, grubby profits identified with a canny North and Industrial Revolution cities like Bradford where, in certain suburbs, so the popular imagination would have us believe, there was a millionaire on every corner, and every town had its 'millionaires' row'.

This is far from the truth. In a region with its manufacturing base in the textile industry, very large fortunes were rare – £30,000-70,000 was typical of a successful manufacturing family, and £100,000-300,000 typical of the richer manufacturers and merchants. To have made more than that amount required outstanding expertise, or possibly the re-investment of profits in another successful enterprise. Of the ninety-two families in this study, perhaps fifteen were millionaires and fifteen half-millionaires, and this approximates to the total for the county as far as new wealth is concerned. Rubinstein's work[20] shows just how thinly millionaires were spread among the nineteenth-century population. Between 1810 and 1909, he suggests that in the whole of Britain a total of 170 men died leaving estates worth £1 million or more, and this total includes landed wealth, old money. Even if we allow that this figure might be revised upwards to take account of such things as tax evasion, death-bed gifts or the squandering of a large fortune, and we multiplied it by ten, even then, the result would be only 1,700 millionaires throughout Great Britain in one hundred years, a minute proportion of the population.

Understanding this wealth structure is important to understanding many aspects of nineteenth-century middle-class life, and more especially, what this study is concerned with, middle-class houses. It is no coincidence, for example, that there might be a marked difference between the houses of families of lesser wealth and those of superior wealth and above. John Deakin Heaton, for example, died in 1880 leaving an estate worth £60,000. By Victorian standards he was a rich man, a well-to-do physician living in Clarendon Road, a good area of Leeds. His house, Claremont, had been built by an eighteenth-century merchant and stood in its own grounds. Heaton had extended the house and remodelled the interior in a Gothic style adding rich plasterwork. By today's standards, we would consider the house large and luxurious. Yet it could not compare with the splendour of Milner Field, the house of Titus Salt jnr, where Heaton and his wife spent a weekend in 1875. Heaton seems to have been overawed by Salt's house, and committed to his diary a goggle-eyed description of the interior. On leaving he wrote:

> We said good bye, and commenced our journey, and in due time we comfortably reached our small and simple looking residence.[21]

23

Although Heaton was an educated man and one who had played a part in the affairs of Leeds, he was on a whole different level to Salt, the representative of a truly wealthy and powerful manufacturing family, with his monumental house full of modern furniture and costly works of art.

Another point worth mentioning in this context is that it was mostly among the higher wealth groups that we find the connoisseurs of art and architecture, men like Benjamin Gott of Leeds who had employed one of England's leading architects to rebuild his house and who had paid for his son to tour Greece and study its antiquities. Abraham Mitchell and Henry Mason of Bradford were other collectors who extended their patronage to promote music in that city and to support young artists. Or there was Swire Smith of Keighley who toured the north of Italy and Venice in the 1870s leaving his textile business for a while and taking up his volumes of Ruskin.[22] Many of these families, then, were a much more complicated mix than the popular imagination will allow. They were not simply a bunch of rich Philistines: among them we find genuine patrons of the arts moving in their own rarified world of super-wealth and business.

However, it would be wrong to think that wealth was the only term in the equation, since family and background exerted a strong influence. Some entrepreneurs never forgot their humble Yorkshire origins, while the rigid religious views of others acted as a check on material prosperity and acquisitiveness. In other words, we are dealing with wealthy *individuals*, people who were divided by as many things as united them. Wealth, family background, education, social responsibilities, religion and politics might all be points of difference. They perhaps explain why a man like S.C. Lister with a good education and a fortunate start in life might become a millionaire art collector with a place in the country and eventually a title, while a man like James Ickringill, who started life as a factory hand, lived in a modest villa near his works despite later wealth. If they appeared to act at times as a group then it was perhaps business and the promotion of a bourgeois ethic of respectability that provided the common bonds of interest that bound them all together into a powerful urban elite.

Nevertheless, some questions were pertinent to them all. How should the industrial magnate view his position in society? What was appropriate to his station in terms of a house? Should he purchase a country estate and pursue the life of a landed proprietor? The chapters that follow are concerned with answering questions like these, and in seeing how far the houses of West Yorkshire magnates reflected the general development of the nineteenth-century house or how far they were modified by local conditions or individual convictions.

CHAPTER TWO
DESIGNS À LA MODE

A Classical Finale

At the beginning of the nineteenth century, if a gentleman wanted to build a house, he would have been faced with a choice of several styles. There were the Classical styles, Palladian or Grecian, as they might have been called at the time, and there were also Italianate, Gothic, rustic, even Eastern styles to muse over. However, despite the variety, most gentlemen would have chosen to build a Classical house, based on the architecture of ancient Greece or Rome. The other styles were often no more than decorative, anyway, and used to embellish forms that were basically Classical. Houses built to Gothic designs, for instance, were rarely faithful to their medieval sources. The scenic value of such houses, moreover, and the desire to merge them with a picturesque scheme of landscaping was often more important than scholarly attention to detail.

For the moment, then, styles other than Classical were of lesser importance, and Classical architecture remained the predominant architecture of the first thirty or forty years of the nineteenth century. And there was good reason for this – by 1800, architects could review a tradition of British Classical architecture stretching back for nearly 200 years. It had begun in earnest with the designs of Inigo Jones in the 1620s and 1630s; it had been subject to Dutch influences; had passed from the drama of the baroque late in the seventeenth century to the dignity of the Palladian villa early in the eighteenth; and it had been revitalised by the neo-classical movement from the 1760s and 1770s. Thus, while there had been changes of fashion and ideology, these had come from within, as modifying influences, and the Classical tradition had never come under attack from a conflicting architectural system. Indeed, neo-classicism had strengthened the position. Broadly speaking, neo-classicism represented a more critical and scholarly study of Classical architecture. It went hand in hand with the view that both society and architecture were at their best when in primitive and simple states. This resulted in the sparing use of ornament, the simple but grand modelling of space, and an architecture of basic, pure forms – the cube, the cylinder, the pyramid. The rediscovery of the architecture of Greece from the 1760s onwards, and in particular the Greek Doric temple, gave a further impetus to the movement and the final stages of neo-classicism are closely bound up with the Greek Revival. The criticism often levelled at neo-classical buildings is that they can sometimes be monumental, cold and severe. This is true of some designs, but in the hands of a capable architect, the results were grand, yet refreshingly simple and subtle.

The first forty years of the nineteenth century witnessed a surge of building by West Yorkshire entrepreneurs, building that was strongly influenced by neo-classicism. But perhaps only two houses can be considered distinguished – Benjamin Gott's Armley House, and Eastwood House, Keighley, built for William Sugden.[1] Gott's house at Armley, near Leeds, was the rebuilding of an existing house by Sir Robert Smirke between 1816 and 1817. It provided Gott with a monumental villa overlooking the Aire Valley from a commanding position. Armley House has been regarded by some historians[2] as the first Greek Revival house in the county, but the actual Greek content of the design is restricted to its giant Ionic pediment. It is its bold proportions and the stark juxtaposition of the wings to the main block rather than the use of Greek detail which produce its cool and sophisticated appearance when compared with other local houses (full description and illustration on pages 148-9). Eastwood House, on the other hand, is firmly Greek. The basic form of the house is conventional enough – a central pedimented section connected at either end to what appear to be pavilions. What makes the house outstanding is the carefully controlled arrangement of windows to create the illusion of pavilions and the application of Greek decorative motifs. The ends of the house stand back slightly from the centre and are treated as two separate units. They are defined by shallow pilasters that frame the windows which are a tri-partite (three light) design with an entablature and blind arch above. What adds to the impression that the ends are separate, is the lack of windows on the first floor in contrast to the centre of the house which has five first-floor windows. This elevation is embellished with panels of key pattern decoration, and each 'pavilion' has, above the eaves, crestings carved with anthemion or honey-suckle motifs. The central pediment contains a wreath, and further accenting is added to the centre with a Greek Doric order portico – amongst the first appearances of this order on a house in West Yorkshire. Eastwood House was built for William Sugden, a Keighley worsted spinner and manufacturer. Local historians of the nineteenth century state that the house was erected in 1819, but some maps[3] show it as existing in 1817. The architect has not come to light, but George Webster of Kendal is a possibility as suggested by Bradford Museum Service on the grounds that Webster designed Sugden's funeral monument in Keighley Parish Church in 1834. However, a closer connection cannot be established.

Few other Classical houses built in the region during the first half of the nineteenth century can compare with these. Buckingham House, Headingley, a large pedimented house built probably for the woollen merchant James Hargreave between 1835 and 1840, comes close, and so does Crosland Lodge, Huddersfield, built probably in the 1820s for

Eastwood House, Keighley, before 1817.

the woollen manufacturer George Crosland. In its subtly worked façade and use of fine ashlar, Crosland Lodge is reminiscent of Eastwood House. However, it has been altered in the later nineteenth century when the north end was remodelled.

Other houses built for the county's magnates during this period range from competent neo-classical villas to semi-vernacular interpretations of neo-classical styles. Many houses dating from before about 1845 can be placed in one of two groups: those with two-storey bay windows as their main architectural feature, or those with straight fronts and a central portico. The first group was at the height of its popularity with entrepreneurs between about 1800 and 1830, although it lingered on in one form or another until the middle of the century. It had emerged probably from designs made fashionable by architects like the Wyatts in the second half of the eighteenth century – such a house had formed the core of Gott's house at Armley before it was rebuilt. The bay windows might be canted or semi-circular; a pair might flank the main entrance, or one might occupy the centre of an elevation. The ornamentation of these houses is usually severe; severely lacking might be another way of putting it, since, true to neo-classical principles, the main interest was in the marriage of forms (here, the cylinder and the cube), decoration being restricted to structural components – columns or relieving arches, for instance. Houses of this type are often built of such fine, closely fitting ashlars that no reinforcement of the angles of the building with corner stones was thought necessary or desirable. Indeed, one of the chief, if austere, delights lies in the finish of the masonry. Quite a number were built: Cabbage House, Keighley, 1780-1800, for the spinner John Greenwood snr; Odsal House, near Bradford, 1795, for the ironmaster John Hardy; Thornton Lodge, Huddersfield, before 1822, for the merchant and manufacturer John Horsfall; Headingley Lodge, Headingley, 1829, for John Marshall jnr; Bowling Lodge, Bradford, 1836, for Edward and Henry Ripley, dyers. All were of the type described, but all have been demolished.

Fortunately, one good example remains: Knowle Hall at Ingrow, Keighley. This house was built between 1800 and 1807 by John Greenwood snr for his son, also called John. It stands on an eminence overlooking the highway from Keighley to Haworth and once enjoyed good views across the Worth Valley from its landscaped grounds. On the entrance front a pair of canted bay windows flank the doorway, each storey of the windows being supported on Tuscan columns. To the south-east front a semi-circular bay of two storeys stands centrally between two relieving arches. This front of the house overlooks the valley and highway and the bay window was probably so positioned to take advantage of the views. Catherine House, or Upper Shibden Hall, was a similar house. It was built around

Knowle Hall, Ingrow, around 1800-1807.

27

Upper Shibden Hall is
a burnt-out shell today.

The tower at Upper
Shibden Hall.
Although an addition,
it is probably of near-
contemporary build.

Bowling House: built in the yard of the Bowling Ironworks *c.* 1798 by J.G. Paley the leading partner, who lived here until 1838. It is now used as offices.

1800 at Catherine Slack, Northowram for the brewer and colliery owner Michael Stocks, and is situated 1,000 feet aloft at the head of Shibden Dean. Again, the bay window was placed centrally and on the front from which the best views could be obtained across Northowram, Halifax and as far south as Huddersfield. An addition was made in the form of a tower connected to the house. This produced a splendidly picturesque effect and on a clear day must have extended the view as far as Lancashire and the High Peaks.

In their day, these were some of the best small neo-classical houses in the region, and they are mostly of one constructional period. Other houses were extended with storeyed bay windows, but the result was not always a happy one. At Oakwood, Roundhay, near Leeds, for instance, the woollen merchant Robert Hudson possibly extended his house in this way, producing a ragged elevation in which the bay windows do not seem to be integrated with the house.

The second group (houses with straight fronts and a portico) were an alternative design. They were usually five or seven bays long with a central entrance. Ashlar or finely dressed rubbles were the favourite constructional material. There is, however, much variation in their quality, an indication that the form was within the reach of the lesser wealthy as well as those of superior wealth – indeed, many of these houses were the first homes of families on the road to greater prosperity. Eller Close, Roundhay, near Leeds, is a good example. This is a house of severe design, completely without ornamentation, the only relief being a band running between the floors and a heavy portico supported on a pair of columns between antae.

Harehills Grove, Leeds.

The house seems to have been built in the 1820s possibly for the woollen manufacturer William Ledgard. Harehills Grove, now called Potternewton Mansion, is more refined, having a segmental portico supported on composite order columns and a tri-partite window above. Its proportions have been carefully considered – possibly by the architect John Clark, who seems to have designed the house in the 1820s for the woollen merchant James Brown. Perhaps the earliest of these houses was Millbank Hall at Luddendenfoot which has a strongly neo-classical front to the east with tri-partite windows beneath relieving arches, and portico with half-fluted Greek Doric columns to the north. The architect is unknown, although the builder and original occupier may have been William Currer of Boy Mill[4] who died in 1807.

This basic form remained popular throughout the second quarter of the nineteenth century, but became more elaborately detailed as neo-classical influences softened during the 1830s and 1840s. Shipley Fields Hall, for example, was built probably in the 1830s for the worsted manufacturer Joseph Hargreaves. It has a Greek Ionic portico, shallow surrounds to the windows and rusticated quoins. Whiteshaw, Denholme, was designed for another worsted manufacturer, William Foster of Denholme Mills. It was built probably between 1840 and 1860, its principal elevation containing an elaborate Roman Doric portico and pedimented windows.

Rebuildings or extensions of earlier houses are commonly encountered. Eller Close, for instance, is the rebuilding of an earlier Georgian house that survives in part to the rear, while at Shipley Fields Hall an eighteenth-century house appears to have been extended and refronted, the original mullioned windows remaining in the rear service rooms. In the last example, traditional detail has been allowed to survive, but the builders of other

Above: Millbank Hall, or Milner
Lodge, Luddendenfoot – notice the
parapet concealing the chimneys.

Right: The doorcase at Millbank
Hall, an early domestic use of Greek
Doric columns partly fluted.

Shipley Fields Hall,
Shipley.

Mill House,
Barkerend,
Bradford: now
demolished, but
built probably
between 1815
and 1822 for the
Garnett family,
worsted spinners.

Ebor House, Haworth.

houses actively pursued this semi-vernacular theme. Prospect House, Queensbury, built for John Foster of Black Dyke Mills around 1827 contains some Classical detail to both front and rear, but it also contains traditional mullioned windows with square surrounds and rubble is used for the walls rather than ashlar. Of course, Prospect House was built at the beginning of Foster's career, but, despite immense wealth later – he was worth at least £250,000 – he continued to live there without significantly rebuilding the house. Similarly, Mill House, Barkerend [D], Bradford had fine detail to the front, but more traditional detail to the rear. Neither house was the reconstruction of an earlier one.

Mill House illustrates the further point that some of these houses are of ill-proportioned or misconceived designs. This is probably the result of a lack of informed architectural guidance, and several houses look as though they have been assembled from pattern book detail by local masons. Thus, at Mill House, while the architectural detail is reasonably good, the lack of symmetry looks odd, and one's first reaction is to assume that the later mill building to the left has consumed the end bay of the house. However, map evidence[5] indicates that the house had always been built like this – that is, as a free-standing structure with an off-centre doorway. Other examples can be found: the brewery house that Samuel Bentley built at Lockwood Brewery, Huddersfield, is a house of squatly Classical proportions; the house near Flush Mills, Heckmondwike, one of the houses belonging to the Firths, manufacturers and merchants, has a decidedly regional appearance, and so does Ebor House, Haworth. The latter was built for Hiram Craven, a contractor, in the early years of the nineteenth century, and was later to be acquired by the Merralls, a worsted family of superior wealth. It represents a vernacular interpretation of neo-classical style.

Above: Meltham Hall, Meltham Mills, *c.* 1841. The house was extended to the left later in the century, unbalancing the original design.

Left: Woodsley House, Leeds, from a mid-nineteenth century photograph which shows the original gates and a balcony to the first floor at the side, detail which has now disappeared.

Built of coarse gritstone rather than ashlar, it has the feel of a Pennine house, especially at the rear, rather than anything from Greece or Rome.

By the 1840s and 1850s, manufacturers and others who continued to build in Classical styles were leaving behind the earlier austerity; elements such as the storeyed bay window as a central feature of the design were also abandoned. However, large, cube-like structures were retained. Meltham Hall, Meltham Mills, was built for the cotton thread manufacturer William Leigh Brook around 1841. The building is vigorously Greek in style with spiky anthemions carved into the capitals of the giant pilasters across the front of the house and similar carving applied in panels to the sides. Centrally, between two pilasters, is a single-storey bay window, looking like a truncated version of earlier work.

The use of giant pilasters at Meltham Hall is similar to the giant Corinthian order applied to the front of Woodsley House, Leeds, built at about the same date as Meltham Hall. The house may have been designed by John Clark for the machine maker Sir Peter Fairbairn. The entablature, balustrade and columns are of stone; the walls of brick. It is unfortunate that brick pilasters were used to terminate either end of the house, since this gives a weak finish to the corners, and there is a top-heavy feeling, generally, about the design. By the 1850s, some large villas, especially in suburban settings, were taking on a different character. Two Bradford houses illustrate this well: Parkfield House and Clifton House, Manningham (illustrated on pages 150-151). Both were the houses of worsted merchants and both were built at the beginning of the 1850s. Their principal elevations have a recessed centre giving the appearance of slightly projecting wings at either side. At Clifton House the portico unites the wings and has a pierced parapet above; at Parkfield House it projects beyond them. In addition, the entrances of both are flanked by single-storey bay windows, a vestige of the storeyed bays of earlier houses. Although it is possible to see the neo-classical origins of these houses, they are, nevertheless, of an indeterminate style, shading into the Italianate designs that were to become so popular locally in the '50s and '60s.

These houses and the others discussed in this section come at the end of a long line of development of Classical architecture. In the main, the entrepreneurs that built them continued the tradition of classicism and were responsive to changing nuances and subtleties of fashion. One thing is striking about such houses as a group: with only a few exceptions they are all small houses, considering the wealth of their occupiers, although they were usually finely detailed, especially on the inside. But they were, nevertheless, at the end of an architectural era, a Classical finale to a tradition which, by the 1850s, was already the subject of much criticism.

The Search for a Style

John Henry Parker was an Oxford publisher as well as a writer on architectural subjects. His *Concise Glossary of Terms* became one of the standard nineteenth-century architectural glossaries, and went through many editions. In the 1846 edition, under the heading of Gothic architecture, he berated Classical architecture thus:

> ... if the Roman Language could neither be preserved everywhere, nor effectually revived, so also the permanent establishment of the Roman architecture was not to be expected. The marvel is that modern Europe submitted so long to its trammels.[6]

In 1849 he gave a series of lectures at Oxford on the history of Gothic architecture, and in the same year had the pleasure of seeing his lectures published under the title *An Introduction to the Study of Gothic Architecture*. Here he went even further in condemning the taste for the Classical:

> Even during the eighteenth century when every kind of taste was at its lowest possible ebb, people still seem to have retained a lingering wish for the imitation of Gothic or Christian forms ... although the architects and builders considered it necessary to repress this taste, and make everything in the pseudo-Greek or Pagan style.[7]

Today such statements sound not so much doctrinaire as downright odd. But in Parker's day and throughout the middle years of the nineteenth century the merits of Classical and Gothic architecture were fiercely debated. The battle of the styles, as contemporaries termed it, was running, and for the most part the goths had the better of it.

Gothic architecture had been present in one form or another throughout the seventeenth and eighteenth centuries, of course. To begin with, numbers of medieval buildings remained, either entire, partly rebuilt or as ruins. Then again, Gothic styles had never been entirely ousted by Classical architecture, even in the eighteenth century. It was, however, often viewed as a style lacking order, and, consequently, attempts were made to regulate it, to bring it into conformity with Classical conventions. Towards the end of the eighteenth century its popularity rose, as it became a style useful for its scenic qualities – its irregularity, its association with antiquity, qualities that fitted well with the more rugged and picturesque approach to landscape design.

By 1800, we can say that there had been a Gothic survival and a Gothic revival. But it was not until the 1830s and 1840s that the tone of this revival was to change, especially through the influence of A.W.N. Pugin, architect, designer, scholar, writer. How much Pugin's thoughts on Gothic architecture were to affect the work of those in tune with the times can be seen from the earlier quotation from Parker where he sets pagan Classical against Christian Gothic architecture, a very Puginian notion. Throughout his publications Pugin had heaped scorn on both Classical architecture and what he saw as sham Gothic buildings employed for scenic effect. He disliked pattern book architecture and architects who worked in a variety of styles. An architect should devote his life to one style, a Gothic style, which was a native style, unlike the Classical which was a foreign style. While Gothic architecture was a Christian form, Classical was pagan, and it was, furthermore, a style associated with sophistication, with the slickness and sharp practice of the town. These were some of the ideas that Pugin promulgated, and in so doing he invested the Gothic Revival with a moral and aesthetic force which it had previously lacked, and one which many Victorian architects were to find attractive.

Very few Gothic houses had been built in West Yorkshire during the eighteenth century or the early years of the nineteenth, and those which had appeared shared some characteristics in common with Classical houses – they were usually symmetrical and built of finely surfaced ashlars, for instance. Others seem to have been built more to satisfy scenic requirements. Cobble Hall, Roundhay, near Leeds, was built perhaps around 1820 as an ornamental farm on the Nicholsons' estate at Roundhay Park. It has walls constructed of cobble with pointed arch windows, but only on the fronts that look into the park where it would have been on view as part of the wider circuit of the gardens, and where it would have harmonised with other garden buildings such as the hermitage and the sham castle which was also built of cobble. But by the 1840s such tricks were out of favour, as a new, high-minded approach came in.

It is difficult to say which was the earliest house in West Yorkshire designed in a convincing Gothic Revival style. Keighley certainly has a strong claim to this honour. Although not strictly part of this study, the presbytery at St Anne's Church had been designed in 1838 by Pugin himself with rather thin Gothic detail, while around 1830-1834 George Webster of Kendal had designed the Elizabethan-style Cliffe Hall for the Keighley lawyer Christopher Netherwood, a house sold after Netherwood's bankruptcy to the Butterfield family. On the other hand, the vicarage at Lindley, near Huddersfield, was also built in 1838, and in an Elizabethan style, but it is a dumpy and provincial-looking attempt. Cliffe Hall is the more interesting since it was built earlier *and* in an already well-developed form possessing several of the design features that were to become standard in later examples – curvilinear gables and an oriel window, for instance. Also, these had been put together in a rather more subtle grouping than some other early houses. Thus, in Headingley, Leeds, a number of Gothic houses had appeared in the late '30s and early '40s, but most were in the former Gothic tradition with symmetrical fronts heavy with sixteenth-century detail grafted onto what was little more than a box planned according to Classical principles – exactly the sort of Gothic deplored by Pugin and those of like mind. Headingley Castle (John Child 1843-46), built for the corn merchant Thomas England, follows this pattern up to a point, but is superior in its well-designed Gothic interior and its entrance tower with oriel window, another element that became an important design feature of the Elizabethan style. Houses of this kind can also be found just down the road from Headingley in Burley. Several were built in the 1840s, although the best is St Anne's Tower built around 1860 for the engineer T.R. Harding.

For most of the county, the 1840s were the date when Gothic Revival architecture – Elizabethan styles in particular – were making their first impact. This was certainly true of Bradford, where the firm of Andrews & Delauney seem to have initiated the Gothic Revival in domestic architecture around 1845 when they designed Daisy Bank at Girlington for the worsted merchant G.G. Tetley. In 1848, the same firm produced a more confident Elizabethan design for the Bradford businessman William Murgatroyd. This was Bankfield at Cottingley to the north of Bradford. Then, in 1849, the merchant John Douglas commissioned a similar design from them for his house, Rosemount, at Manningham. Such houses continued to appear in the Leeds area – Springbank, Headingley, 1860s, probably for the Ellershaw family, oil merchants, and Oak Lea, Adel,

Rosemount House, Manningham, Bradford. A good example of a modest Elizabethan style house, *c.* 1849.

Springbank, Headingley, a house of perhaps the early 1860s. Notice how this old photograph clearly shows the addition of a bay window to the centre of the house.

Woodleigh Hall, Rawdon, was built in 1869 for the worsted manufacturer Moses Bottomley to the designs of the Bradford architects Lockwood & Mawson.

St Anne's Tower.

for William Croysdale, dye-stuff manufacturer, are but two. Woodleigh Hall, Rawdon, is another house that could be added to the group, and one that carries Elizabethan ideas further than several other houses by including in its design those touches of Classical detail (the loggia and portico, for instance) Elizabethan builders often incorporated into their houses. Weetwood Villa near Leeds, built for the banker Henry Oxley, is similar, and dates from 1860-67.

One of the best of these early Elizabethan houses is Bankfield at Cottingley, a tightly grouped design of curvilinear gables with a tower on the entrance front. It is confidently executed, showing how the style had already matured by the 1840s, although one wonders about its provenance – it seems to have been derived from a design published by J.C. Loudon.[8] All of these houses share a rejection of symmetry in favour of irregular, but balanced groupings of forms, usually with gables. In this respect, St Anne's Tower provides one of the more audacious groupings when viewed along its entrance front, for the tower is used to link the main block with the lower service range in a falling arrangement of rooflines. A further characteristic of many of these houses is the use of rock or pitch-faced masonry for walling stone to create a rippling, textured effect when caught in sunlight, and to contrast with the dressed stone used for door and window openings.

Houses like Bankfield or Woodleigh Hall may be more imposing houses than several others built in Elizabethan styles, but they do not reach the palatial proportions of some. Outstanding were Manor Heath, Halifax, and Cliffe Castle, Keighley. Manor Heath [D] was built to the south of Halifax for the carpet manufacturer John Crossley at the beginning of the 1850s to the designs of Parnell & Smith. The house stood on a terrace overlooking landscaped grounds, and was a composition of sloping and stepped gables punctuated by a fine array of tall chimneys and mullioned windows. To the rear, above the service wing, a tower rose with a cluster of chimneys to one side balanced by a high lantern at the other. But Manor Heath could in no way rival Cliffe Castle in respect of towers. Cliffe Hall has already been mentioned. When Henry Isaac Butterfield, the

Above: Cliffe Castle, Keighley: Henry Isaac Butterfield (seated) in the gardens of his recently extended house. Sadly, the house has lost its winter garden and only one tower remains today.

Left: Stoneleigh, Bryan Road, Huddersfield, was built for the cigar maker Edward Beaumont during the 1860s. While there are Elizabethan or Tudor details in the design the architect has freely mixed these with earlier Gothic details, particularly in the porch.

The Woodlands, Upper Batley, 1873, built for George Sheard. The house is now the Bagshaw Museum.

last remaining brother of Butterfield Brothers, a prolific firm of worsted merchants and manufacturers, came into possession of the house in 1874, he set about remodelling it. Henry Isaac seems to have wished to retain the Elizabethan design of the old house, but between 1874 and 1878 employed George Smith to extend it by adding an entrance tower and carriage porch together with a staircase tower and winter gardens. Further extensions took place in 1882 when Hargreaves & Bailey added another tower to the house together with a new music room designed as a baronial hall. When completed, Cliffe Castle was among the largest houses in the county, and stood like a miniature city with its collection of towers, domes and pinnacles.

If Elizabethan Gothic was popular throughout the century, it was not the only style. The Gothic Revival was regarded by some as much more than an architecture based solely on English Gothic buildings. Pugin had commended the Gothic architecture of France, while John Ruskin had drawn attention to the beauties of Venetian and North Italian Gothic. Added to this, indeterminate, mixed styles of Gothic can be seen appearing from perhaps the late 1850s. The battle of the styles, indeed, might well be seen as the battle between different styles of Gothic architecture as much as between Gothic and Classical, and a battle to produce a definitive nineteenth-century style.

The designs chosen by West Yorkshire entrepreneurs during the 1860s and 1870s did not run contrary to these developments. Some houses exhibit French influences in the

Left: Weetwood Lodge, Leeds. The complex grouping of roofs and tower is remarkable. Notice the elongated lucarnes (dormer windows) in the tower roof.

Below: Littlemoor, Queensbury.

use of high roofs – mansard and mitre roofs – while others have chateau-like towers with conical or witch's cap roofs. French Gothic made an impression on a wide range of houses from the suburban villas of the lesser wealthy to the houses of the very wealthy. The villa designed in 1873 by Sheard & Hanstock for the Batley woollen manufacturer George Sheard is a good example, its main entrance emphasised by a short tower with tall French roof.

Weetwood Lodge, Weetwood, near Leeds, was built for the newspaper magnate Frederick Baines between 1870 and 1875. Here, high, sweeping roofs, towers and tracery give an almost fantastic air to the house.

In contrast to French influences, the Gothic architecture of Italy does not seem to have endeared itself to the new rich of the county as a suitable style for their homes even if prominent in some of the region's public buildings or present in much diluted forms in some terraced and semi-detached housing. There is, however, one substantial exception – Bankfield, Halifax, the home of Edward Akroyd. A complete account of the house can be found on pages 157-8, but, briefly, a modest villa on the edge of Halifax was transformed with a Gothic palazzo front during the 1860s by the Atkinsons of York. All of this was in contrast to Woodside [D], the rather cottagey Italianate house of Akroyd's father which stood just a little way down the hill.

European Gothic was not the only influence. Two huge houses were built in a Scottish Gothic or Baronial style: Moorville at Burley-in-Wharfedale, and Littlemoor [D] at Queensbury. They both shared the common features of mullioned windows, rubble walls, crow-stepped gables and towers. Moorville was the earlier and seems to have been built in 1848 for J.H. Whitehead, a Leeds stuff dyer, and extended for Edward H. Hudson, a Leeds worsted spinner and manufacturer.

It was not the only such Baronial building in the area, though: just across the moor stood the Ben Rhydding Hydropathic Establishment designed in a similar style. The two must have made a strange yet complementary pair in the 1850s, set amid the rough pastures and moorlands of Wharfedale. Set at one of the highest points in the Bradford district was Littlemoor, the home of Herbert Anderton Foster, a member of the numerous Foster family of Black Dyke Mills, but one who built a majestic house around 1890. While little is known about the architect of Moorville, Littlemoor seems to have been designed by Thomas and Frances Healey in 1890-91.[9]

While these two houses have a predominantly Scottish feel, they show off other influences as well. Moorville is an adaptation of Elizabethan style, while the architect of Littlemoor freely used Classical detail to enliven his design. Indeed, some architects showed a tendency to mix styles, producing an eclectically varied house. Examples abound, and, again, range through the wealth scale. West Royd, Farsley, was built for John O. Butler of Kirkstall Forge around 1866 by Andrews & Pepper. The Elizabethan detailing of the main house is augmented with a French or perhaps Flemish-looking tower to the entrance. The Butlers were a family of lesser wealth.

William Francis Tetley, the brewer, was in an altogether different league, and commissioned a much more substantial house from the Leeds architect George Corson in 1863. This was Foxhill at Weetwood, Leeds. While the overall form and detail of the house is Gothic, deciding what kind of Gothic is a difficult exercise – there are elements of French Gothic, together with Elizabethan details, as well as a grim, fortified entrance tower. Yet the ground-floor windows of the house have an Italianate feel to them, and there was also a spire, which has now been demolished. To make matters more confusing, an extension in a revived Classical style was made in 1913.

One of the best mixed Gothic houses in the county was Woodlands [D] at Girlington, near Bradford, the home of Angus Holden, later Baron Alston. It was designed by Milnes

Left: West Royd, Farsley, the entrance.

Below: Woodlands, Girlington, built probably between 1866 and 1869.

Milner Field, Gilstead, begun 1871.

& France around 1865. This was a powerful composition whose pivotal point was the entrance tower to which many of the diagonals of the design point, creating a pyramidal grouping of forms. The house was extended by the same architects in 1876 with the addition of a music room which also contained painted glass by Burne-Jones.

Mixed styles of Gothic became common, and the sources that architects drew on can usually be identified. But there were other houses whose design origins were more abstruse. Milner Field [D], Gilstead, was built between 1871 and 1874 for Titus Salt jnr. Although nearly a mile distant from the model industrial village of Saltaire where Salt's mill was located, the grand proportions and elevated position of Milner Field rendered it visible, nevertheless. The house caused some confusion in its day and continues to do so. Firstly, it was built for Titus jnr, that is, the son, not his father, Sir Titus. Secondly, it was designed by Thomas Harris – or was it? A sale catalogue[10] of the house states that R.N. Shaw had a hand in the design, but this cannot be corroborated. Perhaps Salt had approached Shaw, but preferred Harris's drawings; perhaps Shaw had made some suggestions to Harris concerning the house, or made one or two later alterations. As to the style, it was of a muscular quality of Gothic which reminded Linstrum[11] of the work of Burges and Godwin, and which Girouard[12] referred to as 'Wagnerian'. Indeed, anyone would have to think hard to come up with a suitable classification of this style, although *The Building News* in December 1874 roundly defined it as 'Twelfth Century Medieval, which has been strictly adhered to'.

If Gothic architecture seemed to predominate, it never replaced Classical architecture entirely. Indeed, in some parts of the county there were as many Classical buildings as there were Gothic, although in redefined forms of classicism usually influenced by the palace and villa designs of Italy or France. Italianate houses perhaps originated in the work of Nash at the beginning of the nineteenth century. Nash drew on the traditional architecture of the Italian countryside, producing simple, asymmetrical designs. Matters were taken a stage further by Barry who, from the 1830s, derived his inspiration from Florentine and

Longwood Hall, Bingley, *c.* 1867.

Shelf Hall: its demolition was a serious architectural loss to the Bradford and Halifax districts.

Hayfield, the residence of J.C. Horsfall.

Roman palaces of the sixteenth and seventeenth centuries. The Classical orders, arcaded and pedimented windows, broad eaves and campanili all became features of the style, sometimes in symmetrical, sometimes in irregular, but highly pleasing, arrangements.

The first Italianate houses of any consequence began to appear in the region from the 1850s. Perhaps the first design on a large scale was Ravensknowle at Huddersfield, built for John Beaumont, a designer and manufacturer of fancy textiles. It was the work of the London architect Richard Tress and had been more or less completed by 1859, although work on the interior continued into the 1860s – see pages 151-4 for further details. Ravensknowle was soon followed by important designs – Longwood Hall, Bingley, for example. Longwood was built in 1867, originally for W.M. Selwyn, a partner in the Bowling Ironworks, but it was to be occupied by other Bradford entrepreneurs as well, notably the Harrises and Mitchells. While Ravensknowle is in a palatial Italianate style, Longwood Hall is in a quiet, rural style, with plain walling, simple windows, broad eaves and a tower-like entrance with a shallow hipped roof. The architects were the Bradford firm of Lockwood & Mawson who were highly competent in designs of this sort.

One of the most powerful expressions of Italianate architecture was Shelf Hall [D] at Shelf, near Halifax, built in the 1860s for Samuel Bottomley, one of a family of worsted manufacturers. The house was heavily baroque with a pediment to the garden front supported on giant Corinthian columns and with urns and balustrading above the corners of the house giving the impression of pavilions. The architect is unknown, but there are resemblances to the work of the Bradford architect J.T. Fairbank who designed a pair of similar but smaller houses for the brothers Abraham and Joseph Mitchell, mohair spinners of Bradford, at Bowling Park, as the villas were known [D].

Classically based Italianate styles were an important influence that lingered for much of the century. They might also be used successfully to extend houses. There are, perhaps, two principal reasons for this. Firstly, Classical Italianate design might blend well with an existing older house in a Classical style, and, secondly, the irregularity that extensions usually produced might be utilised to create the sort of asymmetrical grouping of forms characteristic of some Italianate architecture. By these means some remarkable houses were brought into being. Hayfield [D], Glusburn, began life probably as a small villa built for the worsted spinner James Hartley, but during the 1870s his partner, John Cousen Horsfall, greatly extended the house. The finished product was more fantasy than house, a complex of forms grouped around a tower, with bay windows on different levels. The architects who extended Hayfield are unknown. It was John Kirk & Son of Huddersfield who carried out similar extensions for the stockbroker F.W. Bentley at his house Rein

Kirk & Sons' drawing of the extensions to Rein Wood, 1900.

47

At Menston Hall, Menston, an older house of 1700-50 forms a centre to which Italianate wings and a tower [D] were added. The work of the Padgett family, Leeds dyers and finishers, 1876-8.

Wood at Lindley. When Bentley bought Rein Wood it was just another small villa, but a series of extensions, completed by about 1900, gave him an Italianate design with tower and varied roof line. Other houses were extended simply in a line. At Whiteshaw, Denholme, the Foster family had acquired a farm above their worsted mill, and, perhaps in the middle years of the century, built a small neo-classical house – probably designed by John Dearden of Halifax – adjacent to the original. Drawings[13] indicate that the Dearden house was extended twice to the designs of the Bradford architects Milnes & France: firstly in 1870 to the east; secondly in 1884 to the west. This last extension removed the original farmhouse and incorporated the Dearden house as the centre of a long Italianate frontage.

The asymmetrical massing frequently encountered in Italianate designs is less common in houses built to designs influenced by French classicism, where symmetry in at least one elevation was demanded. Two houses are worth mentioning in this respect: Belle Vue, Halifax, designed by G.H. Stokes for Frank Crossley in 1856, and Broadfold House, Luddenden, built around 1877 for John Murgatroyd. Belle Vue is the superior and is designed very much in the grand manner of French hotels or town houses of the seventeenth and eighteenth centuries. It may in some ways have inspired Broadfold House built, perhaps, some twenty years later. The architect is not known, but may again have been one of the Dearden family[14] who had carried out much work for the Murgatroyds at their worsted mills in Luddenden. Whoever it was, the carriage entrance of Belle Vue seems to have been used as a model for Broadfold – both have a carriage porch with an elliptical pediment above the eaves containing the family crest.

Malsis Hall is in a different vein, being built in a palatial Italianate style, but with tendencies towards French ornamentation, a style which 'The Builder' had referred to as 'modified Italianate'. The house was built for the half-millionaire worsted manufacturer

Belle Vue, Halifax, 1856: high French classicism for a carpet manufacturer.

Broadfold House, Luddenden, *c.* 1877.

Malsis Hall, Sutton-in-Craven. The earlier house is the pedimented range standing to the left, behind the new entrance front.

Strong Close House, Keighley.

Sutton Hall, 1893, Sutton-in-Craven.

James Lund, at Sutton-in-Craven, well away from his manufacturing base in Keighley. There were two stages in the building: a fairly conventional south-facing Italianate range to which a new, east-facing entrance front and tower were added later to create a rambling house that was more or less complete by 1862. The architect, Samuel Jackson, was a master of this indeterminate style of classicism that shaded into the French, and he was much in favour with entrepreneurs in Bradford and Airedale, from whom he received many commissions.[15] He may well have been the architect of Joseph Henry Craven's Strong Close House [D] at Keighley, for example. Jackson continued working until the end of the century, when, in 1893, he designed Sutton Hall [D] for another worsted manufacturer, John William Hartley. By then, he had transmuted his designs to a northern renaissance style, still based on a free form of classicism, but, as in the case of Sutton Hall, formally organised.

Reappraisals

The Gothic Revival had begun in the heat of the debate about Gothic and Classical architecture. If, by the late nineteenth century, the flames had not been quenched, nevertheless, the fires had grown dull, and a younger generation of architects in the 1870s and 1880s no longer looked to medieval monuments as a source of inspiration for domestic designs, nor were they so ready to reject the Classical. A reappraisal was taking place, and they were turning instead to the traditional buildings of the countryside or market town as more suitable models for a domestic style. There had been many influences along the way, from designers and polemicists like William Morris, to architects like R.N. Shaw and his use of materials such as timber and parget or the revived Classical details he

51

began to use in a style that quickly earned the name 'Queen Anne'. Or there was Philip Webb, a friend of Morris, who had in many ways pioneered the way back to traditional farmhouse and cottage architecture. A further important development was that architects were no longer so ardently preoccupied with that holy grail of the nineteenth century, a national architectural style. Instead they were working in styles that were appropriate to the commission and its location, styles that might be Gothic or Classical, or a mixture of both added to a traditional base. The interiors of these houses were in many ways more homely. Much attention was given to the quality of their fittings and the standard of craftsmanship throughout the house generally. By the 1880s, a widespread revival of traditional or vernacular styles was underway, and the new rich of West Yorkshire were quick to sponsor this new architecture.

Two points are worth bearing in mind. Firstly, while some very large houses were built, the tendency was towards smaller houses of recognisably domestic proportions. Perhaps because of this reduction in size, the lesser wealth group were able to afford houses of architectural merit in their own right, rather than scaled-down versions of grander houses. Secondly, although the use of mixed materials and timbering and designs based on southern farmhouse types became common by the end of the century, a strong favourite was the Northern or Yorkshire Manor House, a style based on the use of local stones with gabled elevations and mullioned windows typical of the sixteenth- and seventeenth-century houses that can be found throughout the Pennines.

An interesting example is Spring Hall, Halifax, built for the worsted manufacturer Thomas Holdsworth in 1870-71. Here, in a square block of a house, rubble walling, gables, mullions, leading and bay windows are combined to provide a convincingly Pennine structure. What is at odds with the design, however, is the tower, a feature that does not marry well with the rest of the house. The architect was W.S. Barber[16] who was designing in what, for the area, was an advanced Vernacular Revival style. It is, indeed, difficult to decide whether Spring Hall is a precursor of the style, or simply a maverick, designed to reflect the origins of the earlier house that it replaced. This had certainly been so at Carr Manor around 1879 when Thomas Clifford Albutt MD, had submitted plans drawn up by E.S. Prior for the extension of his house at Meanwood, near Leeds. There seems to have been some disagreement over the plans concerning drainage, and the house was not finished until 1881-82. Parts of the older house were retained and the new work extended it into a long frontage built of Horsforth stone with Pool Bank dressings, the chief object, according to *The Building News* of 21 July 1882, being to produce a house 'representative of a former Yorkshire manor house of the seventeenth century.'

It was not, generally speaking, until the 1880s that the Vernacular Revival really got underway. Around 1880 Sheard & Hanstock of Batley designed Woodlands at Gildersome in a form similar to Spring Hall, but with detail that is Dutch or Queen Anne in character. This was for George Webster, a Morley woollen manufacturer. Other designs of the 1880s include two Keighley houses, Longlands and Laurel Mount. Longlands was built for Edwin Merrall in 1884, and, strictly speaking, is at Lees, Haworth, where the Merrall worsted empire was located. The Keighley architect J.B. Bailey was responsible for the house which is in a Northern Manor House style of the seventeenth century. The south, garden front works the best with its quiet and dignified use of Jacobean ornament, but much of this was originally hidden from view by a long conservatory. The entrance front is marred by a carriage porch of grossly exaggerated form – a confection of buttresses, rustication, arched openings, pseudo-Ionic columns and scrollwork, topped off by castellations. By contrast, the west garden front, an elevation on view over much of Haworth, is almost featureless. The interior decoration alternates between bland classicism and exaggerated Jacobean. Better by far is Laurel Mount, built for the worsted spinner

Spring Hall,
Halifax, 1870-71.

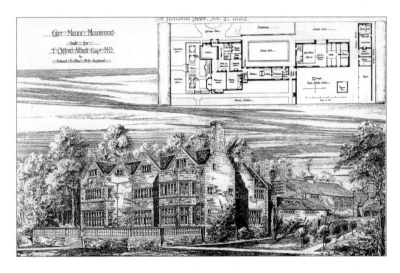

Prior's drawing
of Carr Manor,
Meanwood. It
was built for Dr
Thomas Clifford
Albutt, the
inventor of the
pocket clinical
thermometer.

Woodlands,
Gildersome, 1880.
This engraving
shows the original
house. At the turn
of the century it
was extended in
an identical style
to create a semi-
detached pair of
houses.

There are many solid yeoman farms or small gentry houses of the sixteenth and seventeenth centuries in West Yorkshire, and as some of these came up for sale in the nineteenth century a number were bought by entrepreneurs. Newhouse Hall near Huddersfield is one that was acquired by the Stork family and, although rebuilt and extended, retained much original work. Houses like these were the genuine article that could be refashioned to provide comfortable living.

Ira Ickringill. It dates from 1885 and was designed by A.H. Sugden. The style is a well-handled Queen Anne, but then Sugden was well connected – he was related to William Larner Sugden of Leek, friend of Morris and Shaw. Further details of the house can be found on pages 163-4.

By the 1890s, many new houses were being built in Vernacular Revival styles, although not always successfully, and it is surprising how uncritical some contemporaries could be. Muthesius,[17] writing at the turn of the century, singled out the Leeds firm of Bedford & Kitson as 'a firm of very promising young architects' who had designed houses that were 'among the best works of recent years'. Yet, when one looks at Bedford's Arncliffe (originally Shireoak), Headingley, of 1893, with its half-hearted attempt at a butterfly plan and its thin, weak detailing, or when one looks at Kitson's inept remodelling of Foxhill, Weetwood, resulting in a stunted spire and a bleakly detailed block containing the new library, one simply cannot agree with Muthesius. The firm redeems itself, however, with houses such as Weetwood Croft, a thorough-going Arts and Crafts design of 1896.

Similarly, one must take issue with some of the praise heaped on architects such as Edgar Wood. His best known West Yorkshire work is Banney Royd, the house built in 1901 for W.H. Armitage, a Huddersfield accountant. Again, according to Muthesius, 'Wood is one of the best representatives of those who go their own way and refuse to reproduce earlier styles.' He had 'a great creative power in which a certain poetic gift is dominant.'[18] It was, perhaps, the poet that got in the way of the architect at Banney Royd in 1902. Far from going his own way, Wood came up with a design in a Yorkshire Manor House style, but one that came into conflict with the other elements that he introduced – the entrance porch to the rear, for instance, or the decoration inside which all tended

Weetwood Croft was designed for William George Brown, a stuff merchant, in 1896 and completed in 1898.

Banney Royd, the garden front.

Banney Royd – the main entrance porch to the rear.

towards Art Nouveau. This does not sit easily with such a traditional design of house, and, indeed, looks almost like later remodelling. Nor is the nearby Rosehill (1909) a great deal better. Here, Wood and his partner J. Henry Sellers extended an existing house and modernised its interiors, but the result was a design that lacked refinement – a large box of a house with a red tiled roof and big mullioned windows.

But as with Bedford & Kitson, some of Wood's other Yorkshire designs demonstrate a degree of better judgement – Briarcourt, Lindley, for example, is a more polished Manor House design dating from 1894-95. It is, indeed, rather like an Arts and Crafts reinterpretation of the Elizabethan style so popular a generation earlier. The interior, with its yellow pine panelling, splat-baluster staircase and a frieze by the Lancashire artist F.W. Jackson, shows more than just a painstaking attention to detail and a pride in craftsmanship: here, nothing is exaggerated; all is carefully controlled and appropriate to the design.

Briarcourt, Lindley, from Wood's own drawing and…

… as it is today.

Helme Hall, Helme, from the garden entrance.

Highlands, Burley-in-Wharfedale, was built in 1896 for W.H. Mitchell, director of a local worsted spinning firm. The fire escapes are unfortunate later additions.

It is houses like Briarcourt that are the more successful in the end, for their architects did not so much reproduce earlier styles as reinterpret them, but without resort to extreme stylisations and oddball features. Houses such as Helme Hall at Helme to the south of Huddersfield typify this quieter approach to design. The architect is unknown, but the house seems to have been built in 1887 for Edward Hildred Carlile, a director of the Brooks' sewing thread concern at Meltham Mills. It is constructed of a mellow, grey stone in a style so close to Pennine vernacular that a hundred years of weathering have only blurred the distinction further. Yet it is obviously a nineteenth-century house, planned to nineteenth-century ideas of comfort; modern and showing punctilious craftsmanship in its painted glass or carved oak fireplaces, yet without features that shriek or jar. Other houses in this category would include Highlands, Burley-in-Wharfedale, or Steeton Manor (originally Currerwood) at Steeton, the house of Sir Swire Smith, the Keighley textile magnate. The latter was designed for Smith by W.H. and A. Sugden on a sloping site with a terraced garden to the rear. The house was true to Arts and Crafts principles in many respects, having what the *British Architect* described as all round design, in other words, unlike so many earlier houses it did not have one good front and a poorly detailed rear. In its construction it remained true to local materials – all of the walling stone was quarried on the estate, and the roofs were 'covered with stone or grey slate as was customary in the sixteenth and seventeenth century work of this district.'[19]

But it would be wrong to think that all late nineteenth-century houses followed the Vernacular Revival. Earlier styles persisted – I have already mentioned houses such as Littlemoor, Queensbury, an example of the Scottish Baronial putting in an appearance late in the century, although, again, in a somewhat freer version of the style; and then there were houses such as Samuel Jackson's Sutton Hall, a revived Renaissance style of 1893-94. Other such houses might include Hyrstlands, the house at Batley extended by Mark Oldroyd in 1891 in a style so similar to Sutton Hall that one wonders whether Jackson were the architect here as well. The vernacular might be built into great castellated forms, and there was also a return to a high Classical style. Whinburn at Keighley, built for Prince Smith III between 1896 and 1913, and Heathcote, Ilkley, built for John Thomas Hemingway, in 1906, typify the process (see pages 165-7 and 168-9).

But we have now reached the twentieth century, and this last pair of houses were also the last to be built in the grand tradition of nineteenth-century entrepreneurs. They stand opposed to one another – one in Airedale, one in Wharfedale; the end and the summation of two great themes – one Pennine Baronial, the other Yorkshire Classical. No other houses in West Yorkshire were built on quite this scale after 1914.

CHAPTER THREE
THE WORKINGS
OF THE HOUSE

The large Victorian house was an involved and intricately planned structure. Of that there can be no doubt. Contemporary architectural writers such as Robert Kerr[1] believed that planning had been brought to a state of near perfection in the nineteenth-century house, and one has to admit that in the grand house with its imposing suites of day rooms and collection of service rooms, there was, in Samuel Smiles' words, 'a place for everything, and everything in its place.' Architectural historians have tended to accept this view, seeing the Victorian period as one in which country house owners and their architects were able to plan with optimum comfort and convenience in mind, a state to be brought about by careful attention to numbers of specialised rooms for retinues of servants, and by the successful exploitation of the most up-to-date domestic technology. While this did take place, one or two points are worth bearing in mind.

To begin with, there were few new service rooms created during the nineteenth century when compared with what had been available in the previous century. What we tend to see happening is a more meticulous arrangement and subdivision of rooms. This brings in the second point. It is surprising that, given the contemporary preoccupation with the niceties of planning, Victorian architects introduced little in the way of new plan-forms, but worked mostly within those already known, despite whatever names they might come up with for them. If the West Yorkshire houses in this study reflect these trends, they also show a somewhat simpler approach to planning on the part of the new rich, and they raise a number of other issues.

Plan-Forms

The types of plans available to architects at the beginning of the nineteenth century can be placed into two groups. Firstly, there were the Classical plans, developed by Italian architects and others during the renaissance (figure 1). The most important of these was the villa plan in which rooms were arranged symmetrically around a central hall or saloon. The basic plan was a square or rectangle divided into nine further squares or rectangles with the hall and entrance placed on the central axis, although variations could be worked on this. Next in importance was the double pile plan, derived from the villa plan, where two sets of rooms were arranged one behind the other, again with the hall

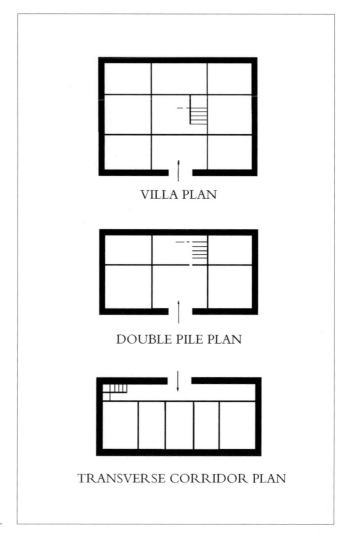

VILLA PLAN

DOUBLE PILE PLAN

TRANSVERSE CORRIDOR PLAN

Figure 1: Classical Plans.

and entrance on the central axis. The transverse corridor plan is not really a Classical form, but, since it seems to have been developed in Classical houses of the eighteenth century, I have included it here. In this plan rooms are entered from a corridor running across the house.

The second group were the Gothic plans. These might be based on great medieval or Tudor houses built around quadrangles or three sides of an open court; or they might be based on designs of houses with an open hall flanked by cross wings. To these plans nineteenth-century architects added the butterfly plan, and free planning. The butterfly plan[2] was largely the work of E.S. Prior and consisted of ranges of rooms set at angles to the house in a Y or X shape. The plan appeared late in the nineteenth century, and was scarcely used in West Yorkshire until the twentieth century. Free planning – a jumble of rooms arranged for convenience – appeared in the county from the 1850s and is of more importance.

Most of the houses built in the first half of the century followed one of the Classical plans. The most commonly used were villa and double pile plans, and whether built on rural sites at the beginning of the century or suburban sites in the middle of the century,

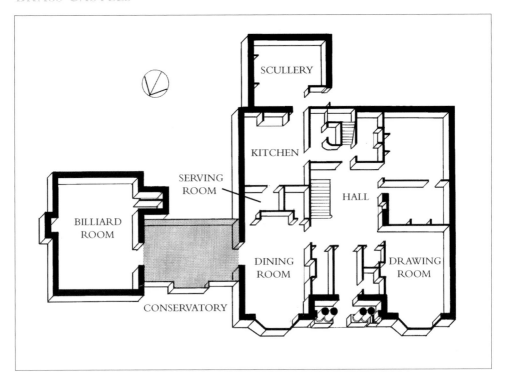

Figure 2: Clifton House, Bradford.

most neo-classical houses were laid out to one of these plans. Clifton House, Manningham (figure 2) was built in the suburbs of Bradford in 1851 and is typical of villa planning; the billiard room linked to the house by a conservatory is an addition of 1863.

Less commonly used was the transverse corridor plan, although it was selected for two of the county's finest neo-classical houses, Armley House, Leeds, and Eastwood House, Keighley. At Armley House Humphry Repton used a corridor running along the rear of the house to connect the wings at either end and to give access to day rooms along the front of the house. The main entrance was at the rear and into a centrally located vestibule. Although Smirk changed Repton's design, the transverse corridor was retained in a similar form. At Eastwood House we see a variation. Here, a central hallway leads to the corridor at the rear of the house from which access to day rooms and service rooms can be obtained, but no rooms open off the hallway itself. Holmefield at Thornes, near Wakefield, was rebuilt with a transverse corridor in 1864, the corridor running from end to end of the house and giving access to day rooms along the south front and service rooms to the north (figure 3).

To say that Classical houses of the first fifty years of the nineteenth century were built to Classical plans is hardly a surprising statement. What is surprising, is the readiness with which architects of the Gothic Revival took to such planning. One of the issues raised by protagonists of the Gothic was symmetry – symmetrical house fronts with symmetrical planning behind was contrary to need and convenience, they argued. Let the planning of the house be considered first and it might be carefully accommodated in the pleasing irregularity of Gothic structure. This, however, seems rarely to have happened. Classical planning around a top-lit hall was common even in Gothic houses. This is understandable in some of the early Gothic houses – Headingley Castle, for instance – which were little

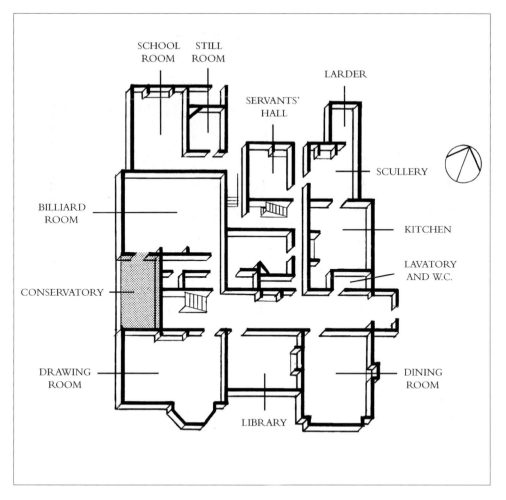

Figure 3: Holmefield, Thornes.

more than Classical villas with Tudor ornament, but it is less easy to understand in some later Gothic designs, especially where big money and a desire to impress went hand in hand.

John Fielden jnr, for example, commissioned the architect John Gibson to build a house at Todmorden for him in 1864. Dobroyd Castle was the result, a vast house set citadel-like above the town and five years in the building. Although designed in a castellated Gothic style, it was planned, nevertheless, around a top-lit saloon to conventional villa planning, the service rooms occupying an adjoining range. Dobroyd is a clear example, but in other houses the villa plan might be modified. Manor Heath, Halifax, was designed for John Crossley by Parnell & Smith in an Elizabethan style. Although the rooms may not be symmetrically arranged within the plan and a number of service rooms have been incorporated to the north-west, nevertheless, it is easy to see how the rooms are set three deep around a central hall (figure 4). Contemporary architects sometimes tried to justify this sort of thing by commenting that it was based on Elizabethan planning, but its derivation is really the Palladian villa.

The above are examples of what one encounters time and again: the adaptation of villa plans to Gothic houses. Indeed, perhaps the majority of Gothic houses built in the

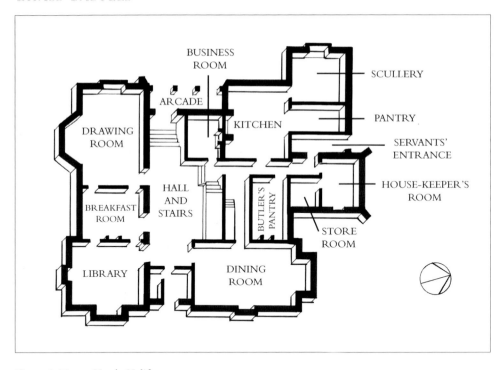

Figure 4: Manor Heath, Halifax.

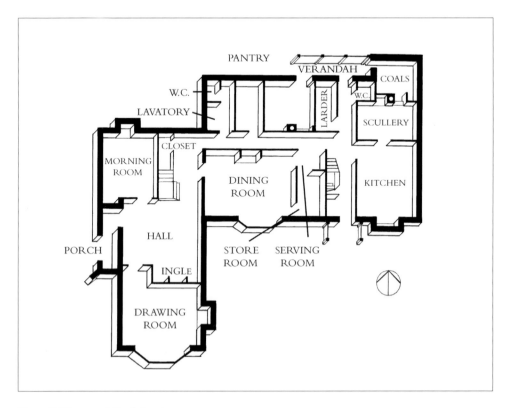

Figure 5: Weetwood Croft, Leeds.

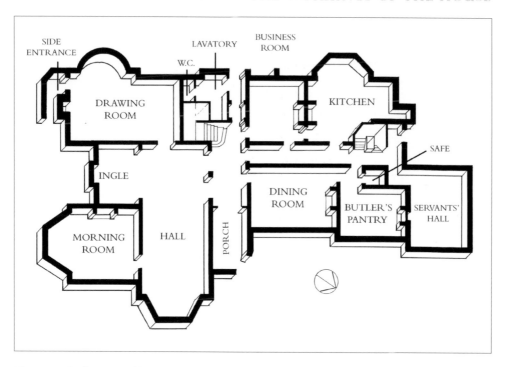

Figure 6: Whinburn, Keighley.

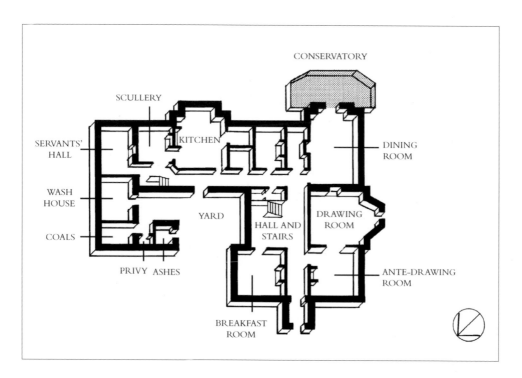

Figure 7: Longwood Hall, Bingley.

county by the new rich employed one form of Classical plan or another, whether it was the villa plan, as at Dobroyd Castle, or the double pile plan, as at Carleton Grange, near Pontefract, rebuilt around 1874, or a transverse corridor plan as at Lockwood & Mawson's 1864 design for Holmefield, Thornes. It is as if it took plan and elevation a generation or more to catch up with one another, and, generally speaking, it is not until the Vernacular Revival houses of the 1880s and 1890s that free planning becomes usual. Then, free planning was most commonly contained within either an L-form as at Highlands, Burley-in-Wharfedale, 1896, or Bedford & Kitson's design for Weetwood Croft, Leeds, of the same date (figure 5); or the house might be freely planned around a roughly central hall as at Edgar Wood's Banney Royd, 1902, or Simpson & Ayrton's redesign of Whinburn, Keighley, 1913 (figure 6).

The Classical houses of the mid-nineteenth century and later – the Italianate and French designs – usually employed Classical planning. But in some houses, especially the asymmetrically grouped Italianate designs, there was a tendency to distort villa and double pile plans to the point where they approached free planning. A good example is Longwood Hall, Bingley (figure 7), shown here in its original plan before alterations were carried out later in the century. Only the two front rooms balance and the rest are asymmetrically arranged, but the plan is clearly derived from the villa plan. Sometimes, however, the Classical house freed itself altogether from Classical layouts. A house like Belle Vue, Halifax, 1857, illustrates the great perversities of nineteenth-century planning, for behind its classically correct French façade lies a freely planned house.

Of the 115 houses recorded, I was able to account for the plans of seventy-seven. Of these, thirty-three were villa plans, twenty-five double pile plans, twelve free plans, six transverse corridor plans and one butterfly plan; yet thirty-eight houses were Classical designs and thirty-nine Gothic designs. In other words, Classical plans make up 83% of the total, yet Classical designs of house account for only 49%. Such study of plan-form in the houses built by the new rich of the county reveals a disjunction between theory and practice. The idea that the Gothic house might bring about a liberation from the symmetry of Classical planning simply did not catch on to the extent that villa and double pile plans disappeared, and the Classical plans, if modified in some respects, continued to predominate. Moreover, while free planning might be found, one is as likely to encounter it in late Classical as in Gothic designs of house.

A Room for Everything

If there was little innovation in plan-form for much of the nineteenth century, a great deal of thought, nevertheless, went into the correct arrangement of rooms within the house. Here, of course, consideration of room function was essential, but that in itself involved a whole range of social niceties. To begin with, most large houses could be divided into four or five zones – rooms for the family, rooms for guests, rooms for the children, service and servants' rooms. It might also be divided by gender – rooms for men and rooms for women; and then by class – areas for polite society and areas for servants. It was this planning in three social dimensions that lead to the elaborate organisation of space we encounter in large Victorian houses.

The house of the magnate, in common with other large houses of the period, had to cater for a variety of needs. The family required their separate rooms in which to relax and to be private. There were frequent house parties and so guest rooms were a further requirement, perhaps with particular rooms set aside for visiting bachelors and so located well away from the rooms where women might sleep. Rooms for masculine pursuits such as billiards or smoking were usual, as were rooms where ladies might take tea with other ladies, conduct their correspondence or give their housekeepers instructions about guests, dinner parties, or other domestic arrangements.

All of this could function only with servants to cook, clean, serve at table, open doors, wash the linen, make the beds, set the fires, run errands, attend to the stables, wash the carriage – the list of their duties is endless. Small Victorian villas or semi-detached houses in middle-class occupation, usually had two or perhaps three servants. Although socially inferior, the servants in such households lived in close proximity to their masters and mistresses because of the very smallness of the house. There was, thus, a good deal of face-to-face contact, and servants were better integrated into the social routine of the family than in the houses of the wealthy. Here, perhaps only the upper servants might be known to the master and mistress, and strict segregation was the rule. For instance, servants should not be found in the best, or day rooms while members of the family were there, unless summoned. They should not be found loitering in the hall unless they were attending to callers. They were restricted to the service rooms usually located to the rear or in a wing attached to the house, and they had their own back ways and routes to take them where their duties required. Understanding this social hierarchy and the segregation of its lower orders from the higher orders that they served is crucial to an understanding of the grand Victorian house. It is clearly reflected even in such simple things as the entrances to the house. The principal front might contain the main entrance for family and guests; to the side or rear was the servants' entrance, and in well-planned houses there was further entrance for taking in luggage.

Inside the house the correct relationship of rooms to one another was of paramount importance. It was also a source of much trouble and endless refinement as far as the writers and critics of architectural journals and other publications were concerned. In even a fairly neutral room such as the dining room (though some thought it should have masculine overtones) many factors had to be taken into account: the room should be rectangular to harmonize with the shape of the dinner table; the relative positions of the fireplace, door and sideboard had to be settled; consideration had to be given to the position of the windows so that the sideboard might be appropriately lit; and this was before the thorny problem of the position of the kitchen, serving room and entrances for servants had been addressed. As Robert Kerr wrote, 'the Dining-room, if it is to be perfect, is probably in every instance the most fastidious in its demands.'[3] At least it was straightforward with regard to the activity which took place there, and it is one of the few rooms that it is possible to recognise today, if plans are not available, since it often contains a recess where the sideboard might be placed.

Kerr also had a good deal to say about the serving of food, the principal considerations being that the food should be warm when it reached the table and that the servants should be seen and heard as little as possible. Things to be avoided were serving hatches and the like which allowed servants' chatter to permeate the dining room, or even allowed them to stare at the guests. Also to be avoided was planning that compelled food to be transported across the main thoroughfares of the house. An ideal arrangement would be to have a service door by the sideboard leading to a serving room usually containing heated cabinets to keep food warm. A private lobby communicating with the dining room was another solution to the problem, and better still, an ante-room or serving room with its own corridor leading to the dining room.

Some of these arrangements could be found in the houses under consideration. Malsis Hall, Sutton-in-Craven, provides a good example, where a pair of service doors leading to a serving room flank the sideboard recess. Above the doors are plasterwork panels depicting fish and game, a hint, no doubt of the treats in store. Malsis Hall is amongst the largest houses built in the county, but similar arrangements can be found in a range of others, from Clifton House, Bradford, 1851, where a serving room intervened between dining room and kitchen, to the first design for Whinburn, Keighley, 1897, where the serving room connected to the dining room opened off the kitchen corridor. Slightly different arrangements were made in other houses, but usually with the same object – keeping food warm and reducing the intrusions of servants to a minimum. At Louis John Crossley's house, Moorside [D], Halifax, a separate lobby with its own hot plate adjoined the dining room; at Weetwood Croft a large recess with serving table was provided next to the dining room and near to the kitchen corridor. In some houses the butler's pantry might be used as a serving room or ante-room between dining room and kitchen. This seems to have been a popular compromise in some smaller houses where space was at more of a premium – Pierremont [D], Bradford, is a good example of this sort of economy where the butler's pantry and serving room were combined.

But there were houses where all the rules were broken. At Cliffe Castle, Keighley, dinner had to cross the main corridor of the house to be brought into the dining room, and this was a common problem in several transverse corridor plan houses – Eastwood House, Keighley, and Holmefield, Thornes, suffered from the same awkward planning. At Carleton Grange, near Pontefract, dinner had to be served via a serving hatch from the kitchen corridor, an operation that might be on view from the hall should the intervening door be left open. At Manor Heath, Halifax, the servants' entrance into the dining room opened from a lobby in which the servants' staircase was located with the kitchen at the end. Manor Heath was built for John Crossley in the 1850s. When his brother Frank came to build Belle Vue in 1856/7, he fared no better, for the dinner wagon and its attendants had to thread their way through a chaos of free-planned rooms before they arrived at the ante-room to the dining room. Worst of all were the houses like Rein Wood, Huddersfield, where dinner had to be trundled across the hall en route from the kitchen to the dining room. It was perhaps at dinner in houses like these that Disraeli is said to have remarked as the champagne was poured, 'Thank God for something warm.'[4]

The position of the dining room was important in relation not only to the kitchen and the serving of food, but also to the drawing room. It was in the drawing room that guests and family would assemble to endure the half hour before dinner, and where the mistress, in her best gown and jewels, had to suffer what Mrs Beeton called, 'the great ordeal' through which she would pass 'with flying colours, or, lose many of her laurels.'[5] During this time she should engage her guests in light conversation 'which will be much aided by the introduction of any particular new book, curiosity of art, or article of vertu.' The half hour over, and dinner being announced, the guests were paired off and the way led to the dining room by the host and the lady he wished most to honour.

Now, the architect's skill was to be put to the test, for the dinner procession and its route was perhaps the only occasion when the strictest formality was observed, even on everyday occasions. On this point, architectural commentators throughout the century were in agreement, although Muthesius[6] seemed somewhat bemused when writing about this aspect of English formality. The route should be a short, but dignified progress across an imposing part of the house and to the dining room. It should not be too near the entrance vestibule, as if the host were showing his guests out again, nor should it, as Kerr put it, 'pass through a door of intercommunication, or slip out of one door and in at the other three or four feet off.'[7]

Here again, theory and practice did not always coincide. At Malsis Hall the drawing room and dining room doors stood opposite one another with a length of hall in between, but dangerously close to the entrance vestibule. At Cliffe Castle H.I. Butterfield and his

The dining room at Malsis Hall showing sideboard recess and service doors.

Above: The dining room at Rein Wood, Huddersfield, early twentieth century. There is a built-in sideboard and circular dining table, sufficient perhaps for everyday meals and capable of being extended on grander occasions. Family portraits are hung on the wall and the room is lit by electricity.

Left: The drawing room at Woodsley House, a photograph of perhaps the mid-nineteenth century. The room is well-endowed with seating, including an ottoman placed centrally.

Above: The drawing room at Littlemoor, Queensbury, early twentieth century.

Right: The morning room at Littlemoor, Queensbury.

Above: Emily Kitson's boudoir at Gledhow Hall, 1890s – a neatly arranged and dignified room.

Left: The library ceiling at Bankfield, Halifax. It contains portraits of Chaucer and Milton (bottom) and Shakespeare and Tennyson (top).

architects committed further architectural *faux pas*: either one passed from the drawing room to the dining room via 'a door of intercommunication', or it was out of one door and in at the other. At Longwood Hall the dinner route led the party from the drawing room, through an ante-room and into the hall (so far, so good), but then straight for a store room before turning sharp right into the dining room. In other houses, however, things were better managed. At Ravensknowle, Huddersfield, the drawing room and dining room stood at either end of a long saloon with a gallery above; at Foxhill, Weetwood, the drawing room and dining room were placed opposite one another across a Gothic inner hall; at Milner Field the party progressed from the drawing room, passed through an ante-room and into a broad corridor where they sighted the dining room at its opposite end. Well planned routes such as these gave an opportunity for display, especially of works of art: the corridor at Milner Field was hung with paintings, while at Bankfield, Halifax, Edward Akroyd conducted his guests from one end of a long saloon, where his collection was displayed, to the dining room at the other end.

The drawing room was considered the most important day room, and, as we have seen, it was the room where guests and family might gather before dinner, and to which the ladies might withdraw after dinner to be joined later in the evening by the gentlemen. But despite this communal use, the drawing room was primarily a woman's room, where the mistress of the house might receive calls from other women and take tea. Here we become aware of the gender division. Further women's rooms associated with the drawing room were the morning room, a sort of sitting room for women, and the breakfast room, where, after breakfast, it might be used to relieve the drawing room, particularly if there were no morning room. Nevertheless, it should, Kerr insisted, 'possess the character of the Dining-room alone.'[8] The boudoir – often located on the first floor – was the inner sanctum, the utterly private room of the mistress.

These rooms had their male counterparts. The library, which had been regarded as a general day room at the beginning of the century, became the principal male day room by the middle of the century. Although books would normally be found there, it was not, as Robert Kerr put it, intended for 'mere study'. A special study might be created, however, off the library. The study, and in some houses the gentleman's 'own room' as

A corner of the study at Rein Wood, early twentieth century.

73

The Library at Wharfeside.

The billiard room at Milner Field, Gilstead – furniture by Jones and Marsh; murals by Fredrick Weeks.

a similar apartment might be styled, was the male equivalent of the boudoir. This was strongly in evidence at Carleton Grange, home of Thomas Tew, banker and well-respected Freemason. The study there contained Tew's Masonic library and was 'essentially a man's room, and, what is more, that of a student. There is no trace of feminine occupation, or even occasional invasion.'[9]

Many houses also had a business room where estate and other business might be transacted and legal documents kept. One of the chief requirements of the room was a position near an entrance, or better still, a separate entrance, so that the comings and goings of tenants did not impinge upon the household routine and its privacy. At any rate, this was the country house function of the business room, but it had other functions for the urban new rich. As local power brokers and the heads of many a charity subscription list, the business room was the place where matters relating to these affairs might be conducted. Writing in 1877 about the house of Sir Titus Salt, the Revd Balgarnie tells us that the great man used his business room at Crow Nest for 'the reception of visitors who called upon him for the transaction of business, or deputations for the presentation of appeals, &c.'[10]

Thus, the ground floors of houses occupied by the county's newly rich families might contain the following day rooms: a dining room, drawing room, morning room and/or breakfast room, a library and a business room. The most problematic of these rooms was the library. While the use of this room as a male day room was quite common, it might in some houses retain its former use as a general living room, especially in households of a more intellectual bent. It might even take on some of the duties of the business room. The library at Wharfeside, the Burley-in-Wharfedale home of the MP and worsted spinner W.E. Forster, catered for both of these functions. His daughter gave a vivid description of it:

> This library was *the* room of the house. Wharfeside never possessed a drawing-room, properly so called. From the first it was in the library that my mother's sofa, her writing table, her flowers and books were all established ... In later times the library was still the family room, as might have been seen by the various tokens of feminine, not to say juvenile, occupations intruding amongst the piles of newspapers, the letters, Blue books, and despatch boxes ...'[11]

In some houses the library was omitted. This posed the problem of what to do with the men, and it suggests that the drawing room might become more of a general living room, with the morning room as the female retreat. In other houses it was the dining room that became the general living room, when not used for dining, a practice frowned upon. Kerr coldly observed that the peculiarities of the household might call for this sort of arrangement; and while Muthesius thought sitting around an inglenook in the dining room 'snug and comfortable', he was a foreigner. Native-born Englishmen disapproved. When Edwin Lutyens visited J.T. Hemingway at Sal Royd Villa near Bradford to discuss the building of Heathcote, he found the living arrangements unacceptable, and wrote a snobbish letter to his wife saying, 'You would have fits ... boots on in the sitting room sometimes used as a dining room and furnished as such ...'[12]

Billiard rooms – not often present in smaller houses – might also be regarded as one of the male rooms. However, the problem with billiards is that it was a game that could be enjoyed by both sexes, and to this end the table might be located in the hall for easy access. Naturally, this was an inconvenient position, and this may be the explanation of the many planning applications made during the century for the addition of a billiard room to the house: not a sudden passion for the game, but an end to encumbering the hall. In cases like these, the billiard room was usually made a part of a male suite of rooms.

In the larger houses of the county such problems did not often occur, and, given their greater scale, more structure might be given to the planning of the ground-floor rooms. This is particularly noticeable in the houses of some half-millionaire and millionaire families. One scheme was to accommodate the principal male and female rooms along one side of the house. Thus, at Milner Field, the library and drawing room occupied the central block on the south front. They were connected by an octagonal ante-room which they shared and from which husband and wife could gain access to one another's rooms, or where visitors might be allowed to wait. The ante-room also opened onto the garden terrace where views over the park could be enjoyed. Similar arrangements could be found at other houses – at Armley House, Leeds, for example; while at Manor Heath, Halifax, the morning room acted as the buffer zone in an en suite arrangement of library, morning room and drawing room. In such circumstances as these the morning room might take on more the character of a family sitting room. But considerations of this sort did not apply at the fiercely masculine Malsis Hall, where the whole of the south side of the old house was taken up by James Lund's male suite of rooms. First was a library which opened into a smoking room which in turn was connected with the billiard room. At Cliffe Castle a male suite was created on the first floor with library and billiard room forming a block to the north-west together with two (bachelors'?) bedrooms and a bathroom; in a circular tower with entrances from the library and billiard room was a smoking room, the view, no doubt, offering 'some better excuse than the mere desire to smoke'. Kerr would have approved.

One important room omitted so far is the hall. Throughout their work both Mark Girouard and Jill Franklin[13] have observed that the function of the hall was changing during the nineteenth century. Previously, it had functioned largely as an impressive entrance apartment. A staircase might be located to the side or to the rear, and there might be a further room, the saloon, also to the rear of the hall which might be used on formal occasions and decorated in a manner appropriate. But from perhaps the 1830s, there was a tendency for the hall to become more of a living area and even a place where guests might congregate before dinner. Moreover, the Gothic Revival and romantic notions of medieval and Tudor hospitality created a fashion for building Great or Baronial Halls, open through two storeys and sometimes free-standing.

While such developments took place in the houses of the nobility and gentry, there seems to have been little enthusiasm for them among the new rich of West Yorkshire. It was far more common for the hall to be retained as an impressive area of entrance and distribution, usually with the staircase located within it. A typical and well-planned example occurs at Headingley Castle. Entrance is into a pretty octagonal vestibule which is heated. Visitors who were neither guests nor friends might wait here before being shown into the house, first entering the hall from which access could be gained to all the ground-floor rooms. A staircase wound its way up to the first floor, and the whole was lit by a roof lantern with Gothic arched lights above the stairwell. To the rear of the stairs was the entrance to the service rooms and the servants' staircase. Although Headingley Castle is a somewhat small suburban house of the 1840s, the same arrangements, in one form or another, are common and persisted in other, much larger houses. The sequence of entrance vestibule/hall/staircase can be found at Ravensknowle, near Huddersfield (1850s), Longwood Hall, Bingley (1860s), Cliffe Castle, Keighley (1870s), Durker Roods, Meltham Mills (1880s), or Hyrstlands, Batley, (1890s). The Baronial Hall was extremely rare. Surviving houses and documentary evidence suggest that possibly the only such hall built in the county by an entrepreneurial family was at Whinburn, Keighley, in Simpson & Ayrton's remodelling of 1913. Free-standing halls were not popular at all, although H.I. Butterfield constructed one in all but name, when he added the new music room to Cliffe Castle in 1880-82.

The new music room at Cliffe Castle, 1880–82. Music rooms are something of a rarity among day rooms, this one doubly so, since it is built as a free-standing Baronial Hall open through its full height.

However, it would be misleading to suggest that the hall never became a living area. The idea seems to have caught on by the 1860s. Foxhill, Weetwood, was built in 1863, and, in George Corson's original design, contained an outer hall that led to an inner hall with a staircase off it, then through to a heated gallery – in effect a great hall – with a large hall window centrally positioned and overlooking the gardens. Dobroyd Castle at Todmorden, completed in 1869, had a two-storey heated hall called the saloon, which was closed off from the staircase and entrance. Both places suggest that a hall so constructed, that is, where entrance and staircase do not intrude, was used as a living room, or at least, a gathering area.

Houses built towards the end of the century under Vernacular Revival influences sometimes incorporated a more homely single-storey hall as a general living area – Arncliffe, Headingley, Leeds (1893), and Weetwood Croft (1896), are both examples of this, and Highlands, Burley-in-Wharfedale (1896), seems to have been another. But whether living areas or entrance areas, halls, saloons and galleries (the terms blur in the nineteenth century), these were places where it was still thought desirable to create an impression. One way of doing this was by a display of paintings, and, no doubt, 'articles of vertu'. Dark photographs[14] of the hall and staircase at Bankfield, Cottingley, for instance, are, nevertheless, clear enough to show that the whole of the wall space was taken up by pictures. Similarly, at Woodlands, Bradford, Angus Holden hung his collection around the hall, while at Bankfield, Halifax, Edward Akroyd's guests were conducted from an entrance vestibule up a marble-lined staircase decorated with pseudo-Roman frescoes to emerge into a saloon bedecked with part of his collection.

The hall might also be the place used for musical recitals. Some families thought it amusing (others thought it vulgar) to house an organ in the hall; this in itself was an impressive sight, but it might also provide instructive entertainment. Things could be

Woodsley House, Leeds: the hall as Classical entrance.

Dobroyd Castle, Todmorden: the hall as top-lit saloon.

Milner Field, Gilstead: the hall as Gothic recital room.

Weetwood Croft, Leeds: the hall as cosy corner.

The vestibule, Bankfield, Halifax. Here the saloon is on the first floor allowing scope for lavish decoration of the vestibule.

Left: Cloakroom with WC located by the main entrance to Weetwood Villa, Leeds.

Below: Bedrooms at Weetwood Villa all opening from the main landing of the house. Behind the point from which the photograph is taken are linen cupboards in a corridor leading to servants' rooms.

taken too far, however, as the case of Thomas Stuart Kennedy shows. He planned to build an organ for his wife in his new home, Meanwood House, and approached the famous German organ-building firm of Schulze & Sons. But the project got out of hand: the massive instrument turned out to be too big for the hall, and had to be located in a purpose-built organ house in the grounds.[15]

One appendage to many halls was the cloakroom, usually situated to one side of the entrance, and preferably supplied with hand basin and WC. In grand establishments, two might be provided: one for men and one for women. Such arrangements have rarely survived into the twentieth century, although one is still in use at Weetwood Villa, Leeds, now Oxley Hall and part of the university's halls of residence.

Bedrooms are a simpler subject. Usually they opened from the main landing of the house, the principal bedrooms having en suite dressing rooms. In large houses a number of small bedrooms might be located at one end of the house for sons or for visiting bachelors. One point worth raising is the location and the use of bathrooms. These had become common by the mid-nineteenth century, but, as Franklin has pointed out, might well be restricted to servants' quarters, bathrooms being considered appropriate to servants, whereas ladies and gentlemen bathed in their own rooms in front of the fire. The West Yorkshire new rich, however, do not seem to have been confined by this convention. While the old attitude to bathing undoubtedly persisted – at Moorside, Halifax, for instance, Louis John Crossley had a bathroom only on the service and nursery floor – many houses had bathrooms and WCs on the same floor as the principal bedrooms. At Milner Lodge, Luddendenfoot, a house of around 1800, a marble bath survives in a small room adjoining one of the best chambers, while at Ashfield, Bingley, a house built for the banker Alfred Harris in probably the 1850s, there was a bathroom on the principal floor,

Remains of the bathroom at Millbank Hall, showing marble bath and washstand. The hole in the washstand top would have been fitted with a removable bowl.

Above left: Kitson's bathroom at Gledhow Hall, complete with its own fireplace.

Above right: Foxhill, Weetwood. The nursery stood above the servants' hall at the end of the range and was given an oriel window.

and a further one was provided en suite with one of the bedrooms. 'Cleanliness is next to Godliness' might have provided a text for many of the entrepreneurial community with regard to their bathrooms. None more so than Isaac Holden. Holden took a very great interest in his health, and bathing was an important part of his daily round – not only did he take two baths a day, but he also had a personal Turkish bath installed next to his billiard room at Oakworth House, near Keighley. One of his biographers described the bathing arrangements at Oakworth:

> In the house there are twenty-eight bedrooms, each fitted with splendid wash-hand basins, supplied with hot and cold water; the various bathrooms are in central positions conveniently available from the bedrooms. There is an abundant supply of hot and cold water, and a shower, a needle, and douche bath to each.[16]

Holden might be considered something of an eccentric in this respect, yet no more so, perhaps, than James Kitson jnr of Leeds, who had a heavily Italianate style of bathroom constructed at Gledhow Hall, the whole encrusted with Burmantofts faience tiles. Cleanliness, decency and order were important tenets of the new rich outlook on life, and the possession of a bathroom was high on the list of desiderata.

The nursery might also be located upstairs, usually at a mid-way point between the best bedrooms and the servants' quarters. It, thus, provided easy access for parents and for the attentions of the nursery staff. Both day nurseries and night nurseries were common, and in some houses the nursery suite might also contain its own bathroom and WC. Little remains of these nurseries today, and one wonders how local families might have had them decorated and furnished. The position of the nursery did give architects the opportunity of using some form of embellishment to mark it out from the service rooms below – very often an oriel window was the means by which this was effected.

This brings us to the question of servants and service rooms. A note of caution has already been sounded regarding service rooms and the assumption that they grew in numbers during the nineteenth century. We must be careful not to make similar assumptions about servants. It is a common mistake to think that large numbers of servants were a normal part of the Victorian household. Wealth and class played the greatest part in determining the numbers employed. Jill Franklin[17], for instance, has shown that in the aristocratic household a retinue of fifteen servants might be considered a minimum, and that one frequently met with far more. This figure, moreover, is for indoor servants, excluding outdoor servants such as grooms and gardeners. Her findings are borne out by Yorkshire aristocratic families. The Earl of Harewood, for example, had a retinue of at least twenty-nine indoor servants according to the Census of 1881, while even well-to-do local gentlemen such as William Busfeild Ferrand had fifteen indoor servants at his Bingley home of St Ives. However, newly rich families rarely employed servants in such large numbers. The Census of households from 1841 provides a useful guide to numbers of servants and their duties. Using this material I was able to find details of eighty-two households[18] and the numbers of servants employed there. The information collected is tabulated below:

Nos Servants	2-3	4-5	6-7	8-9	10+
Nos Households	29	23	22	6	2

Total = 82 households

From this it is clear that the family employing ten servants or more was a rarity, and the typical family seems to have employed between three and seven. These figures do not represent ordinary middle-class homes, we should remember, but the homes of some of the wealthiest people in the county. While the households with ten or more servants (Lister and Hardy) approached landed household sizes and were millionaire households, other half-millionaires and millionaires, nevertheless, appear to have been content with fewer servants, and what is more, all these new rich families were as wealthy as gentle families and some were as wealthy as the nobility. This highlights significant differences between landed and new rich families, differences which I shall discuss further in the conclusion. Of more importance here, is the way in which this was taken account of in the planning of the house.

The most obvious affect this had was a simple rather than a highly specialised, service area. While in some large Victorian houses rooms might be subdivided into more specialised uses – the kitchen might have a separate pastry room together with two or three different larders – and while service areas might be grouped so that the men's and women's departments were segregated, this sort of development was uncommon in the houses of West Yorkshire new rich. The service rooms were usually grouped for convenience and there were fewer of them. Indeed, it is rare to find more than a kitchen, scullery, butler's pantry and servants' hall together with pantry and store rooms, on the ground floor. Slight variations on this sequence might occur – a housekeeper's room might either replace or augment the butler's pantry; at Moorside, Halifax, there was no servants'

Above: The servants at Eastwood House, Keighley, *c.* 1880. This is typical of the number of servants we might expect to find in the entrepreneurial household in contrast to the large numbers in the aristocratic household. Notice the man extreme right – probably the odd-man; he wears a folded paper hat popular with sections of the working class during the century.

Left: The kitchen at Meanwood House (now Meanwood Towers).

The wash house (left) at Shipley Fields Hall, built outside the house in perhaps the 1830s or '40s. It has its own rainwater collection tank to provide soft water for laundering clothes.

hall, but there was a housemaids' room. In some smaller houses, service accommodation might be restricted to kitchen, scullery and butler's pantry with store rooms, although at most houses cellars provided further service rooms, apart from their obvious uses for the keeping of drink. Lamp rooms and shoe-cleaning rooms can sometimes be found listed as part of the cellar accommodation.

Despite this simplified approach to planning, it would, again, be misleading to suggest that all houses followed the same simple pattern. Some of the houses of half-millionaire and millionaire families were much more complicated affairs. At Milner Field, specialisation was evident in the cook's department with a kitchen, scullery, cook's pantry, wet larder and dry larder and a dairy nearby. The service rooms at Dobroyd Castle also illustrate the point: here there was a kitchen, scullery, coal store with lift to other floors, boot and knife-cleaning room, dairy scullery, larder, game larder, pantry, store room, servants' hall, housekeeper's room, butler's pantry and men's and women's WCs.

The principal service room was, of course, the kitchen. This was always a high room to allow cooking smells, steam and heat to rise, and, in the well-designed kitchen, to escape via a ventilator in the roof. Two kitchens, at Milner Field and Meanwood House, were modelled on the Abbot's Kitchen at Glastonbury, being octagonal free-standing structures with louvered ventilators in the roof.

The kitchen contained cast-iron ranges for boiling great quantities of water and for cooking; there were roasting jacks, a heavy centre table and all the lumbering kitchen technology we might expect of the age of steam. Where kitchens survive at all nowadays, they have been converted to modern institutional or hotel use and all sense of the heat and labour of the past has departed.

The other place where volumes of steam were produced was the wash house and laundry. Because of this, the wash house was usually separated from other service rooms

Langley, Baildon, is a large Italianate house of the 1870s. The laundry and wash house is located outside the house (extreme left) near to the double-gabled range that contains other service rooms.

on the ground floor, or, more frequently, located in the courtyard or in a cellar with direct access to the outside. At some places, Weetwood Croft or Longwood Hall, for instance, the wash house and laundry was incorporated into the run of ground-floor service rooms, but could be entered only from the rear yard of the house.

The other service room that most families seem to have found indispensable was the butler's pantry. This was the room in which plate might be cleaned and stored, and often had a strong room within the pantry or adjacent to it. It was usually a small room and, as we have seen, might be made to serve other purposes in some smaller houses. What is interesting is that the provision of a butler's pantry did not necessarily imply that the family possessed a butler. Indeed, few male indoor servants were employed, and many houses appear to have had a staff composed entirely of women. Thus, at Ashfield, Bingley, and at Pierremont, Bradford, neither family appears to have employed a butler, yet both houses contained butlers' pantries. The conclusion must be that the name denoted the activity that was carried out in the room, rather than the position of the person doing it.

So far I have mentioned only indoor servants, but numbers of outdoor servants were also required – gardeners, grooms, the coachman and the odd- or handy man employed to carry out routine maintenance work. The stables have been given little attention by architectural historians in the past, and yet they were an essential part of the large Victorian house, especially if the house were built at some distance from the occupier's place of business. The carriage, moreover, was a status symbol. Not only was it expensive to buy, but expensive to run: a fine pair of horses would be needed, and it might also be embellished with a rich livery or personal crest, for which privilege the owner was liable to tax. At the end of the century, a four-seat carriage and horses might cost £300-350 to buy and equip, with total running costs of £600-650 a year. Grooms and stable lads were employed to look after the horses which needed stabling, and then the carriage required its own house together with a place where it could be washed.

This range of cupboards survives
in the butler's pantry at Whinburn,
Keighley.

The plate safe next to the butler's
pantry at Banney Royd.

Abraham Mitchell's carriage and pair outside Bowling Park, Bradford, *c.* 1890. Mitchell may be the elderly gentleman in the silk hat to the rear of the carriage.

The stable block at Weetwood Villa, containing stables and carriage house and, centrally, harness and mess room with hay loft over.

Left: The entrance to the stable yard at Bankfield, Halifax.

Below: Figure 8: The Stables at Ashfield, Bingley.

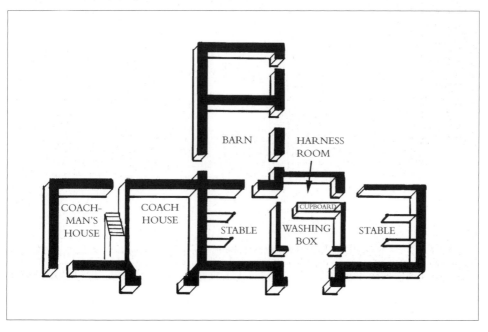

An early motor car house (garage), Heaton near Bradford. This garage of *c.* 1909 is typical of some of those first erected by families of lesser wealth.

Heathcote, Ilkley: the garage designed by Lutyens for the Hemingways.

At large houses a mess room would be provided for the stables staff, and some might even live above the stables or in rooms at one end of the block. The coachman, for example, might live there, although he might well be accommodated at the lodge, a practice that Robert Kerr frowned upon – 'careful men will object to sleep anywhere else than over their horses.'[19] Figure 8, the stables of Alfred Harris at Ashfield, Bingley, shows a common arrangement.

By the beginning of the twentieth century, the motor car was becoming a serious rival to the horse and carriage. Publications such as the year books of the Society of Motor Manufacturers and Traders show that, while there had been getting on for half a million privately owned horse-drawn carriages on the roads by the end of the nineteenth century, by 1910, 53,169 motor cars had been licensed and by 1914 there were 132,015. Motoring writers such as W. Worby Beaumont had demonstrated as early as 1900 that the motor car was more economical to run than a horse-drawn carriage, although this was more likely to be a consideration taken into account by those lower down the wealth scale, where a two-seater car costing around £200 might be a first venture into privately owned transport. It was, indeed, perhaps among the lesser wealth group that the motor car made its first architectural impact, for the new owner of a small car may not previously have been a carriage owner and he, thus, lacked a carriage house which might double as a garage. From about 1900, applications were being made to the building committees of councils for permission to erect 'motor car houses' as the first purpose-built garages were often termed. Along with this came the creation of a new servant, the chauffeur.

It is difficult to say how many of West Yorkshire's newly rich families owned cars at the beginning of the twentieth century. Several certainly did, and what appealed to them about this new form of transport was perhaps less its economy over horse-drawn carriages and more its novelty or the status conferred by one of the expensive, high-powered machines. Occasionally we catch glimpses of the new enthusiasm, as in the letter that Sir Edwin Lutyens wrote to his wife describing the Hemingway family – to Mrs Hemingway the 'motor and motoring are a real joy', while the son had 'a passion for the motor'.[20] Not surprisingly Lutyens designed Heathcote for them with a garage rather than a coach house.

The above describes the types of rooms we might expect to encounter and the problems associated with the smooth running of the large nineteenth-century house. The incorporation of the service rooms into the house was a further problem that faced the architect. Solutions in the previous century had included containing service rooms in a semi-basement with the principal floor above, by locating them in pavilions joined to the house or by positioning them in a block or wing to the rear. While these ways of planning persisted in the nineteenth century, there was much less of a tendency to use basements and cellars, except for storage, and from the mid-nineteenth century service rooms were being combined with the house front and were sometimes decorated in similar ways. At Dobroyd Castle, Moorside and Whinburn, for instance, the service rooms adjoin the entrance front and, externally, are indistinguishable from the detailing of the day rooms. However, the point should not be overstated, for in many other houses areas of service rooms were distinctly demarcated by the use of lower ranges of buildings, inferior positions and plainer detailing than the main house.

A further aspect of planning concerned privacy, for, in the Victorian house, privacy was a prime consideration in the dealings between family and servants. Servants should be at hand when needed, otherwise they should be out of sight. Thus, the service area was linked to the main house by an elaborate system of corridors, separate entrances and back stairs. The principal staircase from the hall to the first floor was to be used only by the family and their guests, and servants were not to be found there except to clean it,

Service or back stairs were often mean and devoid of decoration, but this one at Woodsley House, Leeds, has a graceful simplicity.

The passageway beneath the terrace at Foxhill looking back to the stairs that lead up to the service entrance.

which should have been attended to before the family rose in the morning or when they were otherwise engaged. To gain access to the first floor and to their own rooms above, servants used a staircase located to the rear of the house and running its full height from basement to attics. Servants' own rooms were positioned so that they could not overlook parts of the grounds where the family might take their leisure. At Foxhill there was even a passageway constructed beneath the garden terrace so that servants and gardeners passing from the service entrance to the far end of the grounds could not intrude on the polite society above. Let Robert Kerr have the last word:

> It becomes the foremost of all maxims, therefore, however small the establishment, that the Servants' Department shall be separated from the Main House, so that what passes on either side of the boundary shall be both invisible and inaudible on the other.[21]

The Technology of the House

Technological innovation was the keynote of the nineteenth century and many of the new rich included in this study were themselves innovators. Holden, Lister, Salt, Ripley, Bray, Brotherton, Beaumont, Green and Crossley were all families who had been directly engaged in the development of new technologies or the pioneering of new industrial processes. Other families had taken advantage of and exploited the new industrial technology in making their fortunes. Did they, then, bring a similar attitude of mind to bear on the design of their houses ? The answer is a qualified yes. There are two parts to the subject – innovation in constructional methods and materials, and innovation in the day-to-day running of the house, that is, in its domestic technology.

Least innovation seems to have occurred in the construction of houses. Both architects and their clients stuck to traditional techniques and materials, matters changing only slowly and in line with national trends. Plate glass and Westmorland slate, for example, both began to be used more frequently, but only from the 1850s and following national developments such as the abolition of the duty on glass in 1845 and the development of coastal shipping and the railway system. The basic constructional material of the house remained the well-tried local stone – ashlars and coursed, dressed rubbles for the exterior, undressed rubbles for internal walls. Bricks had been made locally since the sixteenth or seventeenth century, but their uses for inner-skin walls did not make much headway until after the middle of the century, and even in Leeds, where there was something of a tradition of brick building, stone remained the material favoured for the houses of magnates, brick being seen as a cheap substitute. Thus, the typical house was constructed of stone with a cavity between inner and outer walls filled with loose chippings and stones; brick was used only for such things as flue partitions and non-load-bearing partition walls. Floors and ceilings were suspended on deal or occasionally oak beams and joists, and the roof was covered with stone flags until about 1850 or so when Westmorland and other slates came into more common use.

Yet some new ideas were introduced. One was the use of shallow arches springing from cast-iron beams to support ground floors above cellars, the beams themselves sometimes resting on posts or columns. This form of construction could be found in parts of Armley House (1810-20), Lady Royd Hall, Bradford (1865), and Milner Field, Gilstead (1871), and it probably derives from the types of fireproof construction common in factories. Smirke, Gott's architect at Armley, went a stage further, using iron doors in the basement area. Milner Field was important in another respect: it was built with hollow cavity walls to combat damp, a form of construction still uncommon in the county at the time.

The use of concrete was becoming less of a novelty by the mid-nineteenth century, and, indeed, its use for foundations had been advocated by Smirke. By the 1870s, some tentative work in poured concrete construction was being undertaken – Downhill, near Harlow, had been built entirely by this process, and so had a pair of semi-detached houses at Keighley. However, there is little evidence of the widespread use of concrete in the houses of the West Yorkshire new rich, although some later parts of Cliffe Castle seem to have had concrete floors, and Sir Andrew Fairbairn built his new house, Askham Hall, near York, in 1885 on a concrete raft foundation. Despite some modest degree of change, therefore, the approach to building construction remained conservative: new methods were known, but their adoption was slow and piecemeal.

Innovations were more readily made in domestic technology. Perhaps clients were happy to give architects a free hand in the constructional side of the house, but when it came to internal planning and technology, I suspect that there was more client interest. Steam power and heating, hydraulic lifts and efficient sanitary arrangements became a commonplace in the mills and warehouses of West Yorkshire. The entrepreneur was no stranger to such technology, and was perhaps regarded with deference in this respect by other wealthy families. Thus, when Sutherland Walker, the head of a landed family with a house near Brighouse, encountered difficulties in constructing a gas plant near his house, he wrote to John Foster of Black Dyke Mills for advice:

> ... you were kind enough to say one day to Mr Smith [Walker's steward] that you would allow your man to come down and look at my Gas works, and I shall be very much obliged to you if you will let him come to-morrow as there is something wrong and I am afraid the man who has just taken up the contract is going to throw it up.[22]

Iron door in the basement of Armley House. Notice how the metal has been cast to represent a panelled wooden door.

This lift at Whinburn, Keighley, dates from 1897. It is located in the service area and forms the core around which the servants' stair runs.

Central heating could co-exist with Gothic work, as here, where the heating pipes are shielded by a Gothic arcade around the bottom of a hall window – Whinburn, again.

The entrepreneur might put such expertise to use in adding to the comfort, convenience and security of his own home. Security, indeed, was almost a fetish with some families who installed iron shutters that could be closed over windows at night and, by the touch of a button, slid back into cavities during the day. John Beaumont of Ravensknowle had such an arrangement, and they were also in use at Parkfield, Bradford, the home of the merchant Henry Mitchell. This house attracted the comments of no less a person than John Ruskin who had stayed there, and who gave an amusing, if bewildered, account of the gadgetry at Mitchell's house in a letter to his father in 1859:

> New inventions – gas – and cocks and plugs and iron blinds and every conceivable convenience – so that I dared not stir a foot in my room for fear of setting something going and not being able to stop it.[23]

The range of technology installed ran from the essential and workaday to the eccentric. Hot and cold piped water and bathrooms were to be expected by the middle of the century, as we have seen, together with internal flushing lavatories. Gas lighting throughout the house was also common, and was usually supplied by local gas companies. At some houses in rural or isolated positions gas was produced on site – at Malsis Hall, for instance. Similarly, towards the end of the century, one or two houses – Whinburn, Keighley, or Moorside, Halifax – began to generate their own supply of electricity. At Littlemoor, Queensbury, in the 1890s Herbert Anderton Foster had both gas and electricity laid on from Black Dyke Mills, the family business situated about 500 yards away. By the 1880s, telegraphs to mill or office were being wired into a number of homes, particularly if they lay at any distance from the master's place of business. No doubt in these houses a further dimension was added to the business room. There were also gains on the service side. To help make the servants' work less strenuous, hydraulic lifts running from top to bottom of the house might be found in some service areas, thus facilitating the transport of heavy or bulky items such as coals. But hydraulics might be put to more entertaining uses, most eccentrically, perhaps, at Field House, Bradford, the home of the worsted manufacturer Isaac Smith, who had constructed in his hall 'a very large and powerful organ with thirty-two stops, the wind for which is supplied by hydraulic machinery in the basement, under the control of the instrumentalist.'[24]

One might perhaps expect the greatest technological innovation to have been made in the provision of heating, but here tradition and novelty came into conflict. The Gothic Revival house and romantic notions of Olde English hospitality did not sit easily with closed stoves or central heating – a roaring fire was the thing, and what was more, a good deal of showy embellishment might be lavished on the fire surround and the tonnage of stone and marble that supplied the mansions of the county. However, central heating was in use in a number of houses, and was gaining ground by the end of the century, although usually as supplementary heating in the hall and staircase area. At least one house, Bankfield, Halifax, had warm air heating in the hall and vestibule, the heat rising through grills set in the floor.

Two concluding examples of the scale of domestic technology of the nineteenth century might assume and the lengths to which some wealthy individuals might be prepared to go are provided by Louis John Crossley of Halifax and Sir Isaac Holden of Oakworth House near Keighley. L.J. Crossley was one of the third generation of the family of carpet manufacturers of Dean Clough, Halifax. Although he continued to take an active interest in the family firm, it was, to quote a contemporary, 'the study of science to which his predilections have specially turned'.[25] Accordingly, visitors to his house found that 'in almost every room in Moorside there is more or less indication of the all-

Moorside, Halifax – wind and rain gauges and other scientific instruments adorn the roof.

Oakworth House, the principal front after Holden's remodelling. The dome of the winter garden and the two chimneys can be clearly seen in the background.

absorbing pursuit of its owner'. His particular interest was in electricity, and telephones and telegraphs abounded. In the entrance hall was a magnetic clock with a driving weight of half a ton, and in every room there were electric clocks. He had a laboratory and workshop built onto the house in which to conduct experiments with electric lighting and telephony to which end he had several dynamos, and he installed a small electric tramway in the garden. But his most remarkable – some would say bizarre – improvement was the organ. This was a huge instrument, 'somewhat similar to ... the great organ in the Royal Albert Hall', situated between the drawing room and the ante-room to the drawing room, with the front in the former and the keyboard in the latter. A swell organ was located in the cellar with all the necessary pipe work, and to keep it at the correct temperature, the cellar was 'heated with coils of hot water pipes'. Not satisfied with this, louvred openings were made in the drawing room floor to allow the sound to enter from the cellar, 'and consequently when the pedal is applied the volume of tone coming from no visible source has a very pleasing and mysterious effect.' Crossley was also working on an electric action to control an organ in another part of the house, but in 1885 this was 'not yet completed'[26].

Holden was an inventor and a businessman of international standing. He had wool combing works in Bradford and in parts of France, and possessed a great fortune. He was twice married and his second wife preferred life in Yorkshire to life in France. This, coupled with ill-health, persuaded Holden to settle down in the family home at Oakworth. From the 1870s, with the help of the Bradford architect George Smith, Sir Isaac set about the rebuilding of what had been his wife's formerly modest home, creating a stylistically mixed design though one with a heavy French influence. It is, nevertheless, the technology which is the more interesting. To begin with, Holden had installed a telegraph to his works in Bradford, and there was an internal telephone system. We have already seen that he had numerous wash basins as well as bathrooms and a Turkish bath. In addition to this, the house was not only centrally heated, but also double glazed, the temperature being kept at a constant 60° Fahrenheit. Indeed, it is true to say that some form of air conditioning had been introduced, since the air in the house was said to have been changed every half hour, although, according to one relative, not very successfully.[27] In order to heat the house, 7,000 feet of four-inch cast-iron pipes were laid, not forgetting the heating to his glass houses (22,000 feet) and his half-acre winter garden (7,500 feet), a winter garden that was lit in the 1880s by electricity generated at the house. In order to heat the water for this colossal gravity system, a range of furnaces and boilers were required and these had to be kept constantly stoked – Holden's coal bill was said to be £300 a year, the equivalent of a decent middle-class salary.[28] The smoke from these operations was conducted away by two decorative chimney stacks designed like Italian campanili, one of them 70 feet high. The real problem, however, was water consumption, and in order to keep the boilers supplied, Holden had three reservoirs constructed, two being utilised as ornamental water in his grounds, the third occupying a moorland site. As a precaution against fire, five-inch pipes with hydrants were laid from the reservoirs to the house. Alas, all to no avail. Oakworth House burnt down in 1909 and all that remains today are the ruins of the garden, and the portico to the house still bearing Holden's motto:

Extant Recte Factis Praemia

The Rewards of Good Deeds Endure

CHAPTER FOUR
THE GARDEN SETTING

Classical into Romantic Landscape

A t the beginning of the nineteenth century no other gardens in West Yorkshire could compare with the landscapes around Harewood House and Temple Newsam House. Hundreds of acres of carefully tended parkland surrounded these houses, and had received the attentions of some of the finest designers the eighteenth century had produced – Brown and Repton, for example, as well as Woods, White and Loudon. Even the more modest gentry estates might stand in a couple of hundred acres of landscaped grounds, and everywhere among landed society the landscape garden was a most desirable asset and a subtle token of the natural dominion held over the land by noble or gentle families.

Other wealthy groups had seen the advantages of the landscape garden as a place in which to relax and as a mark of wealth. Accordingly, eighteenth-century merchants in Leeds and Wakefield were buying estates in the rural districts surrounding these towns, and began to build houses and to lay out small landscapes. During the nineteenth century some of the wealthier entrepreneurs followed suit. The grounds around these houses were usually smaller than those of landed families of any substance, and amounted to perhaps fifty acres or less. Not surprisingly, the gardens of the first nineteenth-century entrepreneurs continued the traditions of the eighteenth century: a composition of smooth lawns, trees and possibly water or garden buildings. Although the influence of the picturesque movement is evident in the use of more varied plantings, the full ruggedly dramatic approach of the picturesque was rarely adopted. What the owners of these gardens seem to have desired was a pleasant landscape in which to spend their leisure hours, rather than drama or high art.

The first important garden for a manufacturer was that created by Humphry Repton at Armley House for Benjamin Gott. Repton had visited Armley about 1809-10 and had prepared one of his Red Books[1] on the design of both the garden and the house. The house stood on a bluff amid small grounds, but enjoying a great panorama of the Aire Valley. This was a commission that Repton felt uneasy about – he was not used to working for manufacturers, and Gott's mills at Bean Ing, Leeds, stood on the horizon, discolouring the air with their smoke, although as Repton commented, the distance and smoke made them, at least, less distinct. He decided, therefore, that the garden should express 'a command of view rather than of territory'. To this end, plantings of trees and shrubs were established, and an open area of lawn and a terrace was created to the front

View across the grounds at Upper Shibden Hall.

of the house. From here, two prospects came into view. One to the north centring on the ruins of Kirkstall Abbey, and one to the south-east with Gott's Armley Mill as its object. This, Repton considered, retained the air of a rural mill standing as it did on the River Aire, although it caused him some anxiety, because it might prove a constant reminder of business in a place where his client should forget his cares. Repton also expressed the hope that the industrial development of Leeds would not eventually destroy the view altogether, a vain hope in the event.

Repton gave sound advice, and it was advice which would have served as a model for many another entrepreneur establishing a house and garden during the early years of the nineteenth century, so well did Repton comprehend the position of these newly rich families. Upper Shibden Hall at Catherine Slack, Northowram, was built by the Stocks family at around the same time, and the gardens there may be approximately contemporary. The site was harsher and more picturesque than at Armley, being situated 1,000 feet up, above the Shibden Valley. Plantations were established in the grounds, and judging from what remains today, shrubberies were planted near to the house. As at Armley, the view was the thing, and a viewing or belvedere tower was added to the house itself.

At Eastwood House, Keighley, at the beginning of the nineteenth century a calmer design was laid down. The Sugden family had acquired a more or less flat piece of ground with the highway between Keighley and Bradford forming its eastern boundary. To give height and filter the view of the highway, trees were planted on mounds along the eastern edge of the grounds, and clumps of beeches were carefully positioned across the lawn with

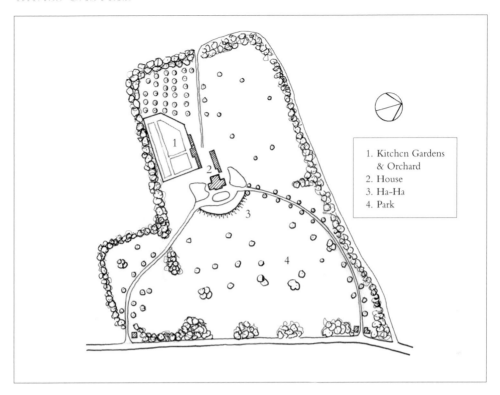

1. Kitchen Gardens
   & Orchard
2. House
3. Ha-Ha
4. Park

Figure 9: Eastwood House.

Eastwood House, Keighley, looking across the park towards the house.

The garden house by the pond at Malsis Hall. It contains a fireplace so that it could be heated on chilly days.

a ha-ha in front of the house providing an uninterrupted view. In common with other small estates, there was an orchard and kitchen garden (figure 9).

The developments mentioned so far had all been completed by about 1825, but the influence of eighteenth-century landscape design lingered on past the middle of the nineteenth century. At Buckingham House, Headingley, James Hargreave had laid out the small area of sloping land to the south of his house with fringe belts and clumpings of trees in a landscape style, perhaps around 1835-40. On a somewhat larger scale, the Foster family created a landscape to the front of their house, Whiteshaw in Denholme, in the 1850s or '60s, a landscape in which their mill could be glimpsed across the pastures. James Lund of Keighley had a large expanse of lawn with dottings of trees around Malsis Hall at Sutton-in-Craven; thicker plantations surrounded the approach to the house where a pond with a garden building and rockwork was also located. This garden was laid out in the 1860s.

Above and below: Milner Field has been demolished and its grounds are used as pasture, but the structure of the nineteenth-century garden has survived.

The grounds at Foxhill near Leeds.

Rock House, Horbury, was built at the beginning of the 1870s for George Harrop a woollen manufacturer. A large Elizabethan house, it was picturesquely situated on rising ground above Horbury looking towards the town across an undulating landscape, while to the west it stood on a crag above the Calder. When Milner Field was being built for Titus Salt jnr at the beginning of the 1870s, he engaged the veteran landscape gardener Robert Marnock to provide designs. Marnock came up with a scheme that showed continuing eighteenth-century influence in some parts, mostly to the front of the house, the Park front, as it became known. But by this date, other influences were at work, also. Indeed, they can be seen in Marnock's work on other parts of the Milner Field estate. The approach to the house, for instance, has a different feel: it is not through park-like grounds, but is hidden from view by plantations of yews and hollies with under-plantings of laurels to create an enclosed and gloomy atmosphere, although this would not at first have been evident. Where the road crosses a little valley on the estate, it is not on a bridge, but an earth rampart planted with further yews. At Dobroyd Castle above Todmorden, although the grounds near to the house were laid out in the 1860s with shrubs and beds by Edward Kemp, the wider view of the house is more striking, for it stands on a wooded and craggy headland, appearing like a citadel from below.

This new and more romantic approach to landscape had arisen because of several factors. The types of Elizabethan and Gothic Revival houses being built in the county from the middle of the century were better suited to woodland settings than lawns and parks of eighteenth-century inspiration. This latter sort of landscape was associated with the very classicism that Gothic Revivalists were hostile towards. Gothic houses and the general medievalising of the mid-nineteenth century demanded a different setting, and one which the charged atmosphere of woodland, crag and cascading stream supplied. The irregular roofline of most Gothic houses was perfectly complemented by the woodland that it broke through to be glimpsed like a fairytale castle. It had other advantages as well.

One of the rustic staircases in the woodlands around Foxhill and the Hollies.

Buckstone House seen amid Crag Wood at Rawdon.

In a part of the country that was becoming more heavily populated, it allowed the house to be on display, but never overlooked, thus preserving privacy. Within the woodland garden, views were internal, so that expanding suburbs and industry could not impinge upon them. Therefore, mature areas of woodland preferably with craggy outcrops on hilly sites or valley sides were in demand.

During the 1860s several such gardens were created. William Francis Tetley probably chose the site for Foxhill because of the extensive views it commanded over the Meanwood Valley and for the mature woodland covering the valley side. The garden to which the terrace at Foxhill once gave access contained walks that passed by great tumbled boulders and ferny hollows, while rustic staircases descended deep into the wood. At the farther end of the valley George William Brown, son of a Bradford worsted merchant, had built his Gothic mansion, the Hollies, adjoining the grounds of the Tetley house. At the Hollies old quarry workings were utilised to dramatic effect, and a similar sort of woodland garden to that at Foxhill was created, but with the notable difference that over the years it was under-planted with countless species and varieties of rhododendron. At Crag Wood near Rawdon similar landscape developments took place. Here a large area of woodland along the Aire Valley became the setting for a number of houses, including Woodleigh Hall for Samuel Bottomley, and Buckstone House for the Dewhirsts, a Bradford family of merchants and manufacturers. Towers and Elizabethan gables broke through the tangle of trees 'testifying more eloquently than words,' as one commentator put it, 'to the wealth and enterprise of the mercantile community.'[2]

Gardens like these were the product mostly of the 1850s, 1860s and 1870s. Few seem to have been created in the closing years of the century. However, small areas of woodland, in effect wild gardens, did become popular. We can see the beginnings of this, perhaps, at Prior's Carr Manor near Leeds, where there is an attempt at a natural fringing of trees to the far end of the garden, and the same thing can be seen at Banney Royd near Huddersfield, where a small area of trees were planted at the far end of the garden beyond the terraces. Much bolder schemes were brought into effect in some gardens. While terraces and formality occupied the front of Sutton Hall, a wooded clough was retained to the north of the grounds as an area of wild garden.

'A Choice Appendage to the House'

Although both traditional and other types of landscape were created in the nineteenth century, it was not the ambition of every newly rich family to possess extensively landscaped grounds. Many were content with a good spread of ornamental garden around their houses, and even where landscapes were created, dressed or ornamental grounds were considered a necessary part of the garden design. Dressed grounds were to be found even at some of the houses built close to or within the factory complex. Benjamin Murgatroyd of Bradford was a partner in the Bowling Dyeworks, and also ran a small soap works at Wood Royd in Bowling. Illustrations show that his house was located next to the works and set in a garden containing shrubs, walks and a small summer house. Murgatroyd, although relatively well-off, could hardly be considered one of the magnates of the region, yet the same scheme of gardening could be seen around the houses of much wealthier people. T.W. Marriott of Wakefield, for example, inherited the family home, Plumpton House at Westgate End. By the time Marriott had finished rebuilding and extending his worsted mills, Plumpton House occupied a central position in the factory complex, with a front garden composed of an informal arrangement of shrubs, and, to the rear, a kitchen garden with glass houses.

Informal beds of shrubs proved a popular way of dealing with the approach to the house and the grounds immediately surrounding it, regardless of changing garden fashions. This was the way that Edward Kemp dealt with the front lawns and the approach to Dobroyd Castle in the 1860s, and it was the sort of arrangement that can be seen at other houses in the county judging from some of the engravings which contemporaries made.[3] But other families desired a more structured garden, and one that reflected the changing shifts in fashion. Changes in garden design and the subtle nuances of fashion in the nineteenth-century garden are a study in themselves. Broadly speaking, it was Repton and Loudon who had reinstated terraces and bedding during the first years of the century. By the 1830s and '40s, quite formal, even geometric arrangements of plants became fashionable, partly as a result of historical revivals – the Elizabethan garden (knots), the Dutch garden (topiary), the French Garden (parterres), the Italian garden (architectural embellishment). By the 1850s and '60s, historical revival was diminishing in popularity, while such features as carpet bedding were increasing. Towards the end of the century, the Surrey School and the influence of the Arts and Crafts Movement were making an impact on garden design. This is a crude analysis, and this is not the place for a discussion of change in the nineteenth-century ornamental garden[4]. However, it is necessary to sketch in some of the details in order to demonstrate how the garden was an essential part or extension of the house itself. As the garden designer Shirley Hibberd put it, 'a choice appendage to the house'.[5]

An important design element in this respect was the terrace. A well-proportioned terrace with a balustrade and steps gave a better architectural base to the house, increasing, as Joshua Major the Leeds landscape gardener observed, 'the extent, importance and richness of the whole.'[6] It might form a promenade in itself and was a place from which the garden as a whole or bedding below might be viewed. It could, furthermore, be embellished with statuary, vases or parterres. The architectural embellishment of the terrace ought to have survived better than any other part of the layout. But while many terraces survive, elaborate examples are hard to find, suggesting that they were never popular among the new rich, although there were some exceptions. The terrace at Milner Field, for instance, showed a degree of sophistication: if its retaining walls looked severe, this was compensated for by the sweeping staircase to the park and the gazebo built into one corner. At Manor Heath a Gothic terrace ran round the house with large heraldic

DOBROYD CASTLE TODMORDEN.

Above and below: This old photograph of Dobroyd Castle shows Kemp's shrubberies around the house when they had matured, and makes an interesting comparison with a similar shot today.

Milner Field, the park front showing terrace, steps and gazebo.

figures set at intervals on plinths. At Strong Close House [D], Keighley, there was a double terrace – a rectangular balustraded one in front of the house with steps down to a further rectangular terrace (see figure 11). These were then set within a large circle formed by the ha-ha which ran around the house, and there were further steps crossing the ha-ha south and west. At Sir Joseph Crosland's Royds Wood [D], Huddersfield, terraces with pierced walls and steps ran around two sides of the garden on the south side of the house. Below was a formal arrangement consisting of a central fountain set in a square divided into four beds. At Sutton Hall there was a double terrace with the steps axially aligned on the entrance front and a rose garden below the second terrace. And at Hyrstlands, Batley, there is still a double terrace with a path aligned axially on the house and leading to a fountain set among rock-work in a shrubbery, although this is now in a poor state of repair.

Most complicated of all were the designs for Steeton Manor and Heathcote, Ilkley. At Steeton Manor (originally called Currerwood) the garden seems to have been designed by the Keighley architect William Hampden Sugden. As shown in his rendering which appeared in the *British Architect* in 1895 (page 291 passim), there was a broad terrace with a parterre laid out with mathematical precision and somewhat reminiscent of Blomfield's work. The terrace at Heathcote was designed by Sir Edwin Lutyens. It has a rusticated terrace wall pierced by three iron balconettes. Below is a geometrically arranged pattern of box-edged compartments filled with flowers, and flanking them are two short canals. Terminating the terrace at either end are summer houses, one with a pergola. They were originally the focal points of two small formal gardens.

Some terraces were far less intrusive architecturally, being no more than grassy banks some distance out from the house. At Sir Frank Crossley's Belle Vue, the house stood on a terrace which was simply a turfed embankment that merged with the lawn. To the west front steps with vases ran down to a fountain and an area of formal bedding. If these embanked terraces seem simple, then they could be built into more complex arrangements as at Cliffe Castle, where steps led the visitor down a double embanked terrace to a semi-formal area laid out with shrubs, bedding and two Italian fountains. In H.I. Butterfield's day the walks along the terraces were lined with vases. At Littlemoor, the

Heathcote, the summer house and pergola at the far end of the terrace.

Ferncliffe, Calverley, the home of a Bradford merchant. The embanked terrace links house with lawn and bedding.

Niche in the terrace wall at Laurel Mount.

The loggia, a place to sit
and look across the garden
towards ...

... the house.

home of Herbert Anderton Foster, the embanked terrace along the garden front had steps
that led to a rockery across the lawn with a covered seat on the periphery. Foster was heir
to the vast manufacturing fortune created by Black Dyke Mills, and came from a family
of millionaire status. This suggests that the embanked terrace was not seen as a cheap or
inferior measure, but as a perhaps more subtle link between house and garden.

The idea of linkage between house and garden became stronger, if anything, under Arts
and Crafts influences. Just how cleverly it could be used is shown by what was probably
W.H. Sugden's design for both house and gardens at Laurel Mount, Keighley. The site
slopes to the east and the house stands on a terrace at the top of the rise with the approach
sweeping around the perimeter of the garden. Steps from the terrace lead to a lawn below
the house and a large niche has been constructed in the terrace wall so that a seat might
be placed inside.

Above and to the south there was a formal garden on the terrace itself with a long loggia
at one end in which to sit and gaze over the garden back towards the house. The terrace,

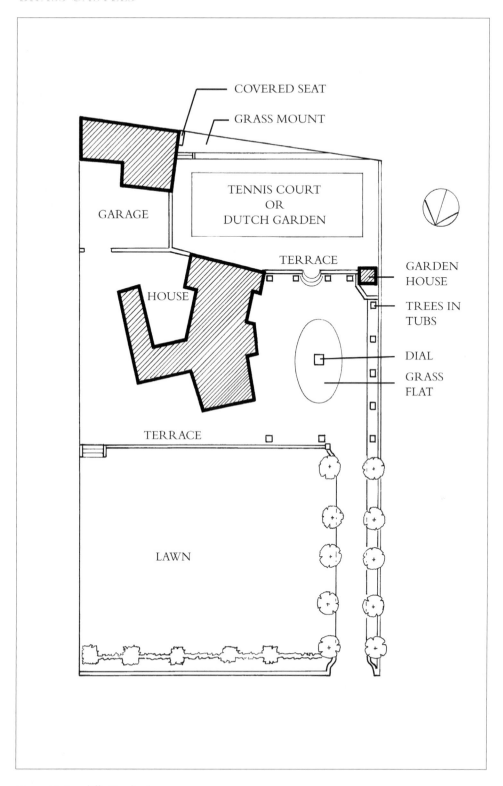

Figure 10: Arncliffe, Headingley.

The summer house on the terrace at Arncliffe.

here, acted not only as a link between house and garden, but as a sort of transitional zone between different parts of the garden as well. This kind of terracing might also work well on suburban sites. At Arncliffe, Headingley, Francis W. Bedford designed a house that stood on an embanked terrace, and as the ground rose to the rear of the house a further terrace was built with a summer house. The terraces mark out three areas: the front lawn, the entrance and the rear terrace or Dutch garden. Bedford's original plan (figure 10) which was altered slightly on execution, shows these arrangements and how the small town garden might be embellished by the use of container-grown shrubs.

Undoubtedly the finest Arts and Crafts garden in the county was created at Whinburn, the home of Prince Prince-Smith at Keighley (see page 165-7 also). The house was first built in 1897 on a steep bank overlooking the Aire Valley. Behind the house were a garden and pond, and to the front was an area of lawn fringed with shrubs and trees. This seems to have been how matters remained until the house was extended in 1912-13 when a new garden was also under construction. The designer may well have been Thomas H. Mawson — his firm certainly redesigned parts of the garden in later years and had worked on other gardens belonging to the Smiths. A grand terrace and staircases were constructed near to the house front and a further series of terraced compartments bounded by clipped yew hedges stepped down the bank, each containing a different scene: a gravelled walk with herbaceous border, a tennis lawn, a long canal with tanks, a lily pond. At the end of the gravel walk is a garden pavilion with a pergola leading up the bank to a summer house from which it was possible to gain views over the garden and the valley in general.

Whinburn, the canal.

View through the remains of the pergola to the summer house at Whinburn.

Whinburn, view along the gravel walk.

Belle Vue, early twentieth century. Although the municipal hand has been at work, the structure of Sir Frank Crossley's garden is still evident in this view taken from the terrace. The Gothic belvedere tower is located centre, back.

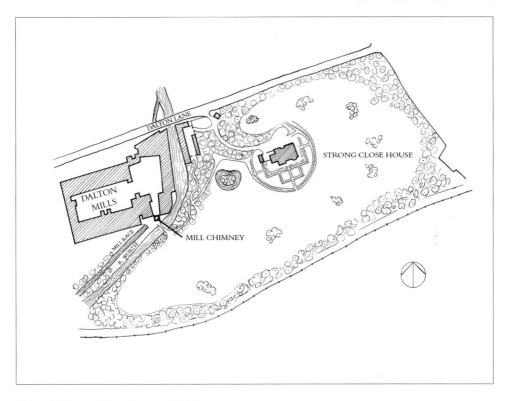

Figure 11: Strong Close House, Keighley.

Terraces, then, were a means of linking house and garden, and a means which proved popular throughout the century despite changes of fashion. Another important aspect of design concerned views from within the garden to the landscape round about. Whinburn is one example; the gazebo on the terrace at Milner Field is another. To the far end of Sir Frank Crossley's garden at Belle Vue a rocky bank was constructed, where, despite the heavy French classicism of the house, a Gothic tower with castellated wall was built. From the tower one could view the whole of the Halifax district. Several houses incorporated a tower into their design from which the view could be enjoyed, but few families had special garden buildings such as the above. The Keighley manufacturers were prolific in this respect. The strangest belvedere of all was that built for Joseph Henry Craven at Strong Close. Strong Close House [D] stood near to his mill in the valley bottom with a sizable garden in a landscape style surrounding it. To gain height in order to view the garden and the countryside, the chimney to the mill was built as the inner core to an ornamental outer casing. Inside, between the two, ran a staircase that eventually gave access to balconies high up the chimney on each of its faces. Its relationship to house and garden is shown at figure 11.

A further aspect of design treated seriously on some estates, although they were few in number, was the linking of house and garden with the wider landscape. This might be effected by the use of distant buildings and eye-catchers. At Malsis Hall, James Lund built a small tower on a ridge of moorland called Earl Crag, a tower that was visible from his garden and on view to the whole of the surrounding district. H.I. Butterfield did a similar thing at Cliffe Castle. During the 1870s and 1880s he added towers to the old Cliffe Hall, turning it into a straggling composition, yet one that was visually united by the towers

J.H. Craven's chimney at Dalton Mills today stands amid industrial dereliction and scrub. Originally, it had a domed ironwork termination.

This view shows the viewing balconies now blocked up.

Lund's Tower, Earl Crag.

themselves. On the northern edge of his garden he added a lodge built as a further tower which answered to the design of the others, thus carrying the visual allusion farther, and to mark Queen Victoria's Diamond Jubilee he built another tower on moorland well to the north of his house. The Jubilee Tower was perfectly sited overlooking the highway to Kendal, and standing like a herald announcing that you were now approaching the Butterfield mansion. Butterfield, indeed, owned a large amount of land between his house and the village of Steeton to the north, and had plans to create a picturesque landscape with garden buildings and with a new approach to the house, but this seems to have come to nothing.[7]

Pleasure and Production

One structure that most houses possessed, usually attached to the house, was the conservatory. It was perhaps Repton and Nash who popularised the connecting of the conservatory to the house with access from one of the day rooms. The conservatory, however, was not a nineteenth-century invention. Glass houses of various kinds had been in existence on the estates of nobility and gentry throughout the eighteenth century. Terminology is somewhat confusing – there was the conservatory, the green house and the stove house or stove, together with a number of specialised houses – orangeries, where tender plants, originally citruses, might be protected over winter; pineries, for pineapples; or vineries. The term stove house usually indicated a heated structure, but then, conservatories might be heated also, and so might green houses. By the end of the eighteenth century a distinction seems to have emerged between the conservatory, which contained planted beds, and the greenhouse, which might be used for bringing on plants or storing plants and small shrubs or trees over the winter. During the course of the nineteenth century the term greenhouse came to be used more and more for a utilitarian glazed house that was part of the gardeners' department. A further complication arose at the beginning of the nineteenth century with the introduction of the winter garden. The idea of the winter garden as a place of public resort, glazed, and stocked with exotic species that bloomed in winter, had probably originated on the Continent. It was soon to become popular in England, but was more usually attached to a house, and was a private garden.

By the mid-nineteenth century it is true to say that the important distinction was between:

1. Glasshouses – utilitarian structures usually situated in the kitchen garden and used by the gardeners for storing and bringing on plants.

2. Glasshouses near to the house that might well be attached to the day rooms.

The latter were always more architecturally structured, might contain potted plants and bedding, and could be embellished with fountains and statuary. Early conservatories usually had walls constructed of masonry, the interstices being glazed. But structures fabricated from slender ribs of cast-iron springing from masonry bases were being introduced from the beginning of the nineteenth century, and by the 1860s had become common.

Whether they should be referred to as conservatories or winter gardens seems to have been a matter of preference. Kerr,[8] for example, regarded size as the only element that differentiated them – when a conservatory exceeded 50 feet square it became a winter

Opposite: The Jubilee Tower near Steeton.

garden.[9] As an illustration of what could be achieved, the winter garden at Oakworth House is a splendid example. The house itself was set on a level site, but land to the rear, where the winter garden was to be built, rose sharply. This was excavated to produce a half-acre site for the winter garden. The far end of the excavation, being mostly of natural rock, formed the end wall of the structure, while the side walls were constructed of composition and natural rock worked into petrified trees and crags. Grottos and caverns were fashioned within these walls and Italian craftsmen laid mosaic floors. The whole was covered over with a domed roof of coloured glass, designed by the Bradford architect George Smith and engineered by Cranstons of Birmingham. To give this vast undertaking more life, mirrors were fitted in the caverns and a moorland stream was allowed to enter the winter garden at the far end and cascade down into a rocky pool before being conducted away. If this were not enough, at night:

> ... the sight is rendered tenfold more delightful ... by the effulgence of the electric light which sheds its rays from six large 'Brush' lamps, lighting up the garden with beams brighter almost than those of the sun, and in which the rushing cascades and highly polished mirrors peeping forth from their framework of delicate foliage and stern rock flash and sparkle again.[10]

Holden's winter garden was entered through the house, and here theory and practice in the matter of conservatories, as with other aspects of planning, were at odds. Some architects thought them desirable, others did not. Kerr was decidedly against joining the conservatory to the day rooms, manufacturing a gobbledegook argument to support his prejudices:

> The warm moist air, impregnated with vegetable matter and deteriorated by the organic action of the plants, is both unfit to breath and destructive of the fabrics of furniture and decoration.[11]

But if Kerr and others thought it undesirable to attach the conservatory to the day rooms, then they reckoned without the doughty Yorkshire constitution. Surviving plans show that conservatories were usually connected to houses built by newly rich families. Moreover, the greatest majority of them were attached directly to a day room without an intervening ante-room, an expedient that Kerr had suggested. Only at Belle Vue and Milner Field was there an ante-room or corridor. At Ravensknowle the conservatory opened from the hall rather than a day room, and John Crossley's conservatory at Manor Heath is a rare example for West Yorkshire, since it was not connected to the house at all, but stood as a great castellated glasshouse on the terrace. Other architects disliked conservatories altogether, a dislike which seems to have been gaining ground towards the end of the nineteenth century. The architect Ernest Newton, for instance, suggested that they were vulgar, 'an outward and visible sign that priceless orchids are grown within.'[12] True; but an accusation that had not been levelled at the eighteenth-century gentry and their stove houses: it emerged only when the new rich could equal the landed class with their botanical collections.

A further question arises, as to its role. Was it a male or a female room? Some Victorian and a number of present-day commentators have tended to the view that it was a female preserve, femininity and flowers possessing an affinity. Thus, it might be used as an extension of the drawing room, and also on those romantic occasions when the bold suitor might propose to the object of his desire. Unfortunately, the cold facts do not bear out any of this. If the conservatory were wholly or even partly a woman's domain, then it ought logically to have opened off one of the female day rooms. This did

The quadruple-domed conservatory at Ravensknowle. It did not marry well with the house, but was an unusual and impressive design. It has now been removed.

happen at some houses. At Laurel Mount, Keighley, it led from the drawing room; at The Beeches, Keighley, from the morning room; at Carleton Grange, near Pontefract, from an ante-room to the drawing room as well as directly from the morning room. However, attachment to the women's rooms did not constitute the majority, for it might also be attached to men's rooms. At Clifton House, Bradford, the conservatory formed the link between dining room and billiard room; at Holmefield House, Thornes, it was positioned between the drawing room and the billiard room, but could be entered only from the billiard room; at Rein Wood, Huddersfield, it adjoined both the billiard room and the male lounge; at Malsis Hall, Sutton-in-Craven, it was part of the male suite of library, smoking room and billiard room. A few houses had more than one: Cliffe Castle had two, while at Pierremont, Bradford, the Priestman family solved all difficulties by having three – one to the dining room, one to the drawing room and one to the library. Our sentimental notions about the Victorian conservatory are in need of modification. Clearly it was a place where tea might be taken and proposals of marriage made, but it was also a place where a magnificent show of exotics might be on view from the dinner table, or a place to conduct one's guests after dinner, or somewhere to lounge, to watch the antics round the billiard table from a distance while one enjoyed a cigar or a glass of brandy.

The Victorian conservatory should be regarded more as a day room, and like other day rooms it had its own servants – the gardeners. In common with the other servants, they were expected to go about their tasks invisibly. All the watering, rearrangement of plants and general maintenance had to be carried out when the room was vacant. They would carry out a good deal of the propagation, also, such was the variety of plants and flowers that might be found in the conservatory – aloes, roses, azaleas, ferns, palms, clematis, passionflowers, geraniums – the list is endless. Some might be container grown and the containers sunk into beds, while others might be grown directly in beds, not counting the potted specimens which might be arranged on staging contemporary prints and photographs suggest that the conservatory might be crammed with plants, or sparsely planted to make room for tables, chairs and other furnishings.

Few original conservatories have survived the nineteenth century. This small example is at Hyrstlands, the Batley home of Sir Mark Oldroyd and dates from around 1891.

The interior of the conservatory at Milner Field, Gilstead, a spacious design for Titus Salt jnr.

The conservatory at Littlemoor, Queensbury, ran along the side of the house with access from one of the day rooms. Notice the open window in the end wall – no fear of deteriorated air here.

Chapel Allerton Hall, the epitome of the well-planned Victorian garden. There is a grand promenade along an embanked terrace lined with specimen plants in pots, bedding is cut into the lawn and to the far right is a range of glass houses, stocked, no doubt, with exotics. This was the house and garden of John Barran, the clothing manufacturer.

But if the gardeners did most of the work they certainly did not do it all: the choice and types of plants grown were decisions for the master or mistress. Gardening, in fact, was a popular hobby, and for the new rich it was a distraction from business cares, although one that might bring them into a certain amount of competition. It was common for head gardeners to be instructed to submit their best plants and blooms to horticultural society meetings. At the Bradford Horticultural Society Exhibition of 1857, for example, the *Bradford Observer* reported that several of the prizes were taken by local entrepreneurs – Daniel Peckover and John Marshall of Leeds won prizes, along with Ellis Cunliffe Lister and Isaac Smith of Bradford; Titus Salt's gardener took prizes for orchids, heath plants, balsams, tender and hardy annuals, black grapes and 'an orange tree in bearing'.

The Salts are a good example of a family who took a great personal interest in the products of their hot houses. Sir Titus had bought the small gentry estate of Crow Nest near Brighouse in 1867 where he had lived for a number of years previously. He seemed content with the old house itself, but added a number of glass houses. His main conservatory contained 'in a recess, an elaborate rockery and cascade, of French workmanship'.[13] His other glasshouses contained fruit, especially one type:

> the banana was his special favourite at Crow Nest, and it attained dimensions rarely met with in this country. Its luxuriant foliage, immense height, and gigantic clusters of bread-fruit more resemble those of a tropical than of a temperate clime.[14]

He also took an interest in orchids, an interest that became an obsession with his sons Titus jnr and Edward. At Milner Field Titus jnr had laid a great amount of land under glass partly for the raising of orchids. Edward's house at Baildon, Ferniehurst [D], was frequently visited by collectors and gardening journalists eager to view his orchid houses. The *Gardening Chronicle* informs us of the breadth and beauty of Edward Salt's collections:

> FERNIEHURST – Some time ago I paid a visit to this place, the residence of E. Salt esq., whose extensive collection of orchids has frequently been noticed in these pages. My object was more particularly to see a plant of the now well-known *Oncidium macracanthum*, with a spike 12 feet long bearing 44 flowers![15]

The Odontoglossum House at Ferniehurst was considered a model of perfection containing numerous orchids – there were 150 plants of *O. Alexandrae* alone.

Besides pleasure grounds, conservatories and hot houses, no self-respecting gentleman would be without a kitchen garden. All the country houses of the nobility and gentry had them, but they were less frequently found at the houses of the new rich. This was perhaps partly due to suburban locations or to the small grounds which some houses possessed. Only the larger estates tended to have a kitchen garden. On the other hand, the growing of fruit was something owners of both large and small estates seem to have found desirable. Vineries, pineapple and melon houses could be found in greater or lesser numbers at the houses of many entrepreneurs, even where the kitchen garden proper was absent.

While many houses have survived, the gardens that once surrounded them have mostly disappeared. This is hardly surprising, since the garden is the most transient, the most fragile of forms. Many gardens have simply been sold for building land and swallowed up. Others have been laid out with brash new schemes that do anything but enhance the setting of the house. As I write, I can think of others where the bones of good designs lie waiting to be broken up or buried – ranges of derelict fruit houses, decaying garden buildings, smashed and dry fountains and kitchen gardens with scrub and trees growing out of them. It is a matter for regret.

CHAPTER FIVE
BUSINESSMEN OR GENTLEMEN?

There are two popular beliefs concerning nineteenth-century magnates, especially those from the North of England. The first holds that factory owners usually built a house close to their factory where, despite hoarding up great riches, they continued to live humbly and continued to display vulgar manners and habits of mind. The second maintains that, if not fathers, then sons were quick to retire on the profits of industry, buying a country estate and settling down to live the lives of landed gentlemen. Both, I believe, are caricatures, yet like many popular beliefs, they encapsulate an element of truth. The purpose of this chapter is to explore the limits of these caricatures by posing the question whether the successful entrepreneurs of nineteenth-century West Yorkshire should be regarded as unpolished businessmen, or whether they had aspirations to become landed gentlemen? Or whether, indeed, such categories are sufficient to describe a new and complex social grouping?

An observation worth making is that throughout the eighteenth century the ambition of those social groups whose aspirations had a chance of becoming reality was towards gentility; and that a mark of gentility was the possession of a country estate and a house appropriate to that position. The outlook is caught well by Dr John Simpson, a young physician from a Knaresborough family who had set up his practice at the beginning of the nineteenth century in Bradford, a place he loathed. In 1825 he recorded in his journal:

> Feb 1st ... I am particularly partial to a country life and rural sports & hate the bustle of a town, particularly the coarse, rude bustle of a manufacturing town ...
>
> I have a small estate situated between Harrogate & Knaresborough which I would take into my own management & indulge my tastes for rural pursuits at the same time that I might improve the land and increase the income derived from it.[1]

What prevented Simpson from doing this was fear of offending his uncle whose heir he was. But after the death of his uncle in July of 1825 Simpson was able to realise his dream.

It is difficult to find similar ambitions on the parts of West Yorkshire's nineteenth-century industrialists. What many seem to have wanted from *their* houses were places in which to relax with their families and to be private. The location of the house should be at some distance from the business, yet within easy reach of it. At the same time, many seem to have wanted a house built so as to express their superior wealth and standing. Such preoccupations can be found time and again in the letters or private journals of contemporaries. The position is well summed up in Humphry Repton's advice to Benjamin Gott on the situation of Armley House:

> The villa is supposed to be the occasional and perhaps only summer retreat of those whose engagements do not permit of a permanent residence in the country; and whether it be the villa of a Prime Minister, or the Merchant, its character supposes seclusion from intruders with a command of view rather than of territory ...[2]

In other words, this was not the home of the great landowner, but a rural retreat, a term often used to characterise such residences. Here, for instance, is one journalist writing about Bolton Royd, a Greek Revival villa built in the 1830s for a Bradford manufacturer. It was a house 'which could offer a great charm to a gentleman wearied during the day with the incessant clack of the loom', but one which lay 'within a convenient distance from his business.'[3] This was a consideration taken into account when Angus Holden, another Bradford entrepreneur, was fixing on the site of his new house, Woodlands. As he wrote to his father in 1865:

> I have bought Mr Thomas Hollings' estate just above Daisy Hill side, since my return ... It is a good position for a house, and quite sufficiently in the country to be nice, and near the town, on which account it will be very convenient as also for being near the works.[4]

Favourite locations, then, were at some distance from towns and places of business. If we look at the borough towns of the region towards the end of the century we can see that there had been an avoidance of the centres of towns by the middle class as locations for residence and the creation of middle-class suburbs on the edges of towns instead, as well as a move to more isolated rural areas. In Leeds this occurred to the west of the town at Headingley; in Bradford to the north-west at Manningham; in Halifax the movement was to the south, towards Skircoat; in Huddersfield it was to the north-west towards Edgerton. A similar pattern reproduced itself in Dewsbury and Keighley.

But unlike the majority of the middle class, the new rich possessed carriages and could afford to move even farther out of towns. Thus, in Leeds, the move to rural areas north of the town begun by merchants of the eighteenth century, was continued during the nineteenth century as mansions began to appear at Roundhay, Weetwood, Meanwood and Adel. In Halifax the far side of Skircoat was colonised by the Crossleys, while Thornes and Sandal to the south of Wakefield became the places where several entrepreneurial families settled down. In Huddersfield, the far side of Edgerton towards Lindley and Birkby was accessible to those with carriages. At Bradford some of the more northerly townships became desirable places to build houses, especially as communications began to improve — Shipley, Baildon, Apperley Bridge and Rawdon were all within reach of the town. Along Wharfedale, the towns of Menston, Burley and Ilkley occupied a special position, being popular with the entrepreneurs of both Leeds and Bradford.

Thus, two locations for house building proved agreeable to the new rich: suburban sites, or rural sites somewhat isolated from the suburbs. It was in these situations, particularly the more isolated ones, that the men of business built their Classical villas or Elizabethan manor houses. They surrounded them with walls, guarded them with lodges and gate-keepers, and, on the face of it, appeared to live the lives of very private country gentlemen. But this was not so. Unlike the landowning class which depended on income from land, the new rich depended on income from business, and the houses they built in the locations discussed above had scarcely any land attached to them, relatively speaking. They were simply good homes in quiet locations, with business only a carriage ride away.

But if the majority of newly rich families preferred a rural or suburban location for their houses, there were other families who ran against the trend. Some lived close to their places of business, even within the factory complex itself. The Cloughs of Keighley, the Rands and Garnetts of Bradford or the Marriotts of Wakefield all provide examples of this at some point in their careers. It is true, however, that later generations of these families bought or built houses well away from their factories, and it is possible to argue that first generations did not have the money to lavish on fine houses or stylish living while they were establishing their businesses. This argument is difficult to rebut and, in any case, is probably true of a number of people. But we should remember that there were also those who built houses located away from business premises in the first generation – John Beaumont of Huddersfield or Benjamin Gott of Leeds spring immediately to mind. We must also remember that several entrepreneurs were wealthy enough to have moved away from their business locations, but did not. Thus, a man like John Clough of Keighley was a rich man, leaving a fortune of £60,000 when he died in 1865. Although I have categorised this as lesser wealth, it was wealth, nevertheless, in Victorian England. Yet Clough died in the mill house at Grove Mill, Ingrow. Nor was this sort of thing restricted to lesser wealth. The Hagues were a family of Dewsbury woollen manufacturers and bankers of superior wealth. John Hague snr lived at the mill house near Dewsbury Mills, while his partner, and later his son, lived at Crow Nest, the somewhat grander house that he owned. Samuel Eyres was a millionaire woollen merchant and manufacturer, yet lived at Hope Villa, Armley, a small house just across the road from his mill at Winker Green.

A related phenomenon is the cluster of houses built close to a mill and occupied by several generations of the same entrepreneurial family. Thus, with one exception, the Holdsworth family of Shaw Lodge Mills, Halifax, lived in houses built within 250 yards (220 metres) of their mill (figure 12). Yet the Holdsworths were a family rising from lesser to superior wealth. They were also local philanthropists, and one became Mayor of Halifax, another was a noted art connoisseur. Similar developments occurred at Haworth where the Merrall family concentrated their worsted business in two mills, building houses close by (figure 13). One house retained by them as a residence was the vernacular-looking Ebor House. The last house they built, Longlands, was located at the top of a bank virtually on a level with the chimney of Ebor Mill, situated at the bottom. Yet this was a family of money and influence. So were the Fosters of Queensbury, with two millionaires in the family, yet we can see three generations of building within approximately 500 yards (450 metres) of their mills – Prospect House, 1820s, Harrowins House [D], 1850s, and Littlemoor [D] and Park House, 1890s. Although other members of this very large family lived at some distances from the mill, it was those most actively engaged in running the business – and the wealthiest – who built the above houses.

In all, some seventeen of the families in this study lived within 500 yards (450 metres) of their mills or factories, and a further eleven had at some time in their lives lived in houses that were within the factory boundary, although they may later have moved to more salubrious surroundings. However, seven of the eleven retained their factory or mill houses as life-long residences. This information is summarised in the table below, which suggests that just over 30% of families had at some time lived either in a factory house or in close proximity to their factories – a minority, but one to be taken account of. What the table does not reveal is that in every case the families were engaged in manufacturing industry. There appear to have been no truly wealthy merchants or bankers in West Yorkshire living over the shop.

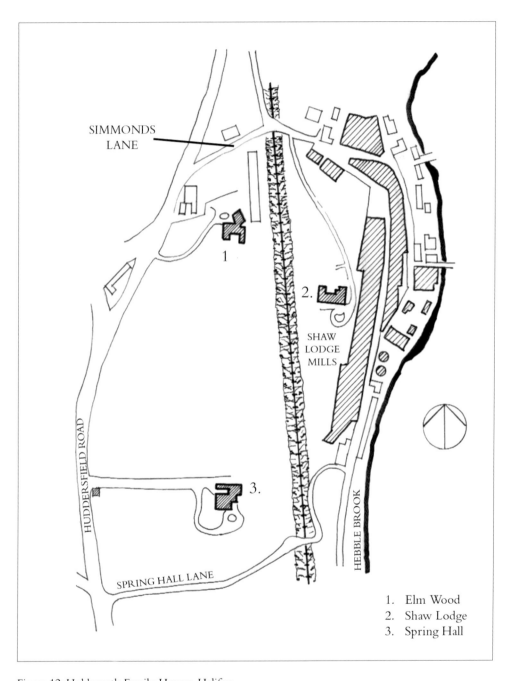

SIMMONDS
LANE

SHAW
LODGE
MILLS

HUDDERSFIELD ROAD

HEBBLE BROOK

SPRING HALL LANE

1. Elm Wood
2. Shaw Lodge
3. Spring Hall

Figure 12: Holdsworth Family Houses, Halifax.

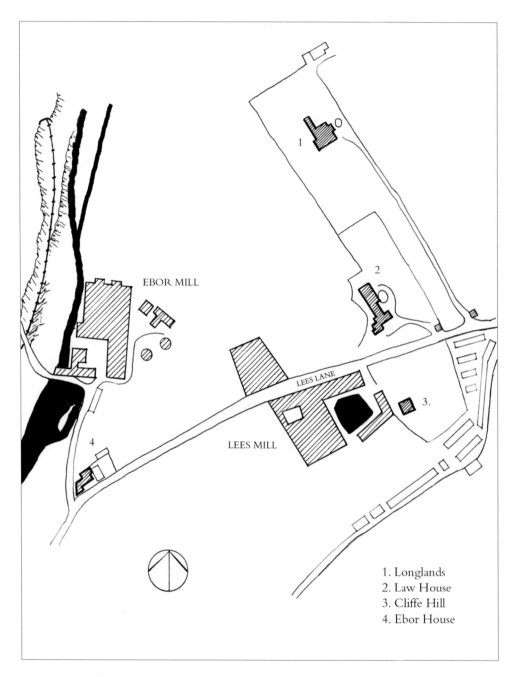

Figure 13: Merrall Family Houses, Haworth.

Within 500yds/450m		Within Factory		Ditto Retained	
No	% total	No	% total	No	% total
17	18.5	11	11.9	7	7.6

Family Residences near to Factories (Total = 92)

It is difficult to come up with the reasons why such families persisted in building so close to their factories when they possessed sufficient means to build in more fashionable or more rural areas. Nor is it clear why these developments should be restricted to manufacturers. There was, perhaps, some virtue in locating a house close to the factory, when it was part of a model village, for as Disraeli wrote of Mr Trafford, the enlightened factory owner in his novel *Sybil*, the entrepreneur should 'comprehend his position too well to withdraw himself with vulgar exclusiveness from his real dependants'. Thus, at Akroyden near Halifax, the house of its founder, Edward Akroyd, is situated on a bank to one side of his model village; although, in truth, both Akroyd's house, Bankfield, and his father's, Woodside, pre-dated the village, and stood, originally, within a short distance of the factory.

What is more, contemporaries – as far as it is possible to judge– seem to have viewed such developments with an equanimity that seemed to border on contradiction. Thus, in 1879, the author of the revised version of William Keighley's *Keighley, Past and Present* could write:

> Nearer the town is the Elizabethan seat of Mr E.D.A. Marriner. In a few years the more advanced growth of the surrounding shrubs and trees will complete the attractions of this admirably situated villa, and render it the most striking object in the landscape. In the valley beneath lies the ornate abode of Wm L. Marriner Esq., J.P.

From this description no-one would suspect that Worthville, the house of E.D.A. Marriner, was built within 400 yards (360 metres) of the mill, and Greengate House where W.L. Marriner lived was within the mill complex. Yet the same author acknowledges the need for other entrepreneurs in the district to build houses away from the factory chimneys of Keighley.

Modest houses are perhaps the result of the firmly held religious principles of other families which prevented a show of pride and materialism. Such principles may be the explanation of the simple lifestyle of James Ickringill, a worsted spinner of Keighley. A fervent Primitive Methodist, he lived in an extremely modest house close to his works and filled the space between the two with houses for his workers. He contributed liberally to charities and built a mission hall across the road from his house. Although he had a second home in Heysham, it was, again, a modest dwelling, and he was to found a convalescent home next door. On the other hand, the unquestionably sincere beliefs of Sir Isaac Holden, a Weslyan Methodist, did not stop him building a remarkable house at Oakworth and acquiring a chateau in France. In fairness, Holden's conversion to materialism may have come later in life. A series of letters written by his son Angus complains of the Holdens' first home in France and the shabby nature of its furnishings.[5]

Whatever interpretations might be put on all this, there was undoubtedly a minority of new rich who conformed to the popular belief of men who never forgot their humble origins, or, indeed, revelled in them. A mild example is John Reddihough, the son of an

Oxenhope farmer. Although he amassed a fortune of above £1.5 million dealing in wool waste on the Bradford market, he built himself a fairly unassuming – considering his immense wealth – villa at Baildon, and it was said that he 'remained a Yorkshireman of simple habit and speech'.[6] William Murgatroyd of Yeadon is a more extreme example. He lived in Yeadon most of his life, where, like his father, he became a woollen manufacturer eventually building Moorfield Mills on the edge of the village. Murgatroyd was worth £295,500 when he died in 1921, yet he had lived all of the latter part of his life in a small house adjoining the mill. In Yeadon, where he was known as 'Billy Murg', he had a reputation for Yorkshire bluntness. When once asked how he should be addressed, he is reported to have replied: 'Well it's like this 'ere. When I'm in London it's Sir, and when I'm in Bradford it's Mr Murgatroyd, but when I'm in t' mill it's – "T' owd b...'s back again"'[7]

The position must be subjected to careful scrutiny: while around 20% of families in the study lived within a short distance of their factories, only 11 or 12% lived against the factory gates and the majority of these moved away to other houses at some time. A mere 7–8% continued to live at factory or mill houses and they were mostly first-generation entrepreneurs. Although the view of the Yorkshire industrialist as a man who retained his vulgar origins is not without foundation, it has been exaggerated in the popular imagination.

The other set of circumstances to be considered is the acquisition of second homes and country estates by newly rich families. In fact, quite a number of families either built or bought second homes – thirty-six out of ninety-two, or 39%. This raises the question of whether such newly rich families were attempting an entry into landed society – the counterpart of the previous view. By and large, this was not so. There are several reasons other than social advancement why a second home might be thought desirable. For many it was a symbol of wealth, a mark of their standing, and more than that, it provided a place in which to relax at holiday times and at weekends, too. Other families seem to have regarded the purchase of country estates as a business proposition, an investment in land, as much as an investment in status. Eric Sigsworth[8] has demonstrated very ably how members of the Foster family bought country estates for such purposes. While later generations of the family may have made marriages into landed wealth, investment seems to have been the object of earlier generations. Although John Foster senior may have lived out part of his retirement at Hornby Castle near Lancaster, one wonders, really, what the old man found to do in this great pile of a building. Not surprisingly, he made regular trips back to Queensbury where he died at his old home, Prospect House.

A consideration in this respect is the amount of land owned by newly rich families, for often their so-called country houses had only gardens around them and little else in the way of an estate. When John Bateman's *The Great Land Owners of Great Britain and Ireland* is consulted, many of the newly rich families who possessed country houses are not listed, because the amounts of land they owned were trifling. Bateman lists only seven. Of those seven, the acreages of their estates and the rents which accrued to them were mostly in the range of 3,000–5,000 acres with rentals of £5,000–£9,000 annually. Of course, these were very considerable sums in nineteenth-century terms, but they put the newly rich landowner on a level with middling gentry only – compare them, however, with aristocratic or wealthy gentry estates. Harewood brought in £38,118, Temple Newsam £45,491, W.B. Beaumont of Bretton Hall could reckon on £34,670, while Sir George Armitage of Kirklees brought in £17,064.

The locations of second homes are also revealing. The majority were located in either the North or East Ridings of Yorkshire, especially near Harrogate and Ripon, or in the North West from Southport to the Lakes. In other words, within reach of the railway centres of Leeds and Bradford. However, this point should not be forced. Some early

Lunefield, Kirkby Lonsdale, Cumbria, the country place of the Bradford banker Alfred Harris. The house was designed for Harris in 1870 by Alfred Waterhouse. There was a forty-acre park, but no estate.

Swinton Castle and Park, Swinton, near Masham, North Yorkshire. The acquisition of this estate had cost S.C. Lister £400,000. In 1879 he owned 24,569 acres in the North Riding, and was to add to this holding.

acquisitions such as those of the Marshall family in the Lake District were made before railway lines were extended to those places, and would originally have involved a lengthy journey by carriage. On the other hand, a number of houses were second homes only and should not be thought of as country houses – five families had houses in London, while seven others settled down to retirement at seaside resorts such as Bournemouth, Torquay, Morecambe and Southport, leaving the strains of business to younger generations.

But, again, the popular imagination is due a certain amount of respect, for a minority of families undoubtedly sought social advancement in the acquisition of a country estate. S.C. Lister of Manningham Mills, Bradford, for instance, who, while he remained in control of his business interests until his declining years, bought Swinton Hall in the North Riding.

He also bought the neighbouring estates of Jervaulx and Middleham, making him a substantial landowner. In 1879, his estate income amounted to £17,253, rendering him equal to the barony that was conferred on him in 1881. The Hardies of Low Moor acquired a London and two country houses, probably to give weight to their political aspirations as much as anything. Chilham Castle in Kent and Dunstall House in Staffordshire became the power-broking bases of the Hardy clan who supplied three Conservative Members of Parliament. The third, Gathorne Hardy, was created Viscount Cranbrook for his services to the party. However, the family retained their business interests in the Low Moor Ironworks, and also their previous home, Odsal House, built close to the great ironworks itself.

Very few families abandoned trade, as the Greenwood family of Keighley did. They had risen from a Pennine yeoman clothier background in the eighteenth century to a position of prominence as cotton spinners by 1800. They had built a couple of good houses in Keighley and during the first half of the nineteenth century had bought the Swarcliffe Hall estate at Birstwith not far from Harrogate. They built a cotton mill there, also. By the mid-nineteenth century, the family had more or less severed its ties with Keighley and its industry, and had retired to Swarcliffe Hall which they rebuilt and enlarged in a Gothic style. John Greenwood, born in 1829, had been educated at Eton and Christ Church, Oxford. He became MP for Ripon and lived on his country estate at Swarcliffe, having demolished the cotton mill at Birstwith, the last visible link with trade. The income from his estates was between £9,000 and £10,000 annually – at the bottom end of the landowning range, but sufficient to establish him as a country gentleman.

For sheer, naked social climbing, however, few could equal the Greens of Wakefield. Edward Green snr was an ironfounder and engineer who had invented a fuel economiser, an invention that laid the foundation of the family fortune. This was to be put to good use by his son, Edward jnr, in advancing the family socially. He became Conservative member for Wakefield, was awarded a baronetcy and developed an interest in field sports. By 1880 he had bought an estate in Norfolk where he built a country house, Ken Hill, adjoining the Sandringham estate of the Prince of Wales whose company he and his son Lycett Green cultivated. The Greens had also bought the Treasurer's House at York to which the Prince was also invited, and he and Lycett had become involved in a royal scandal over a game of baccarat. Frank Green, Sir Edward's youngest son, took charge of the business, while Lycett worked hard at becoming a country gentleman. 'His job was to ride the family into Society', as one of the family put it.[9]

It is not possible to quantify the individual desires and social aspirations of all the people in this study. But it is worth pointing out that even a family like the Greens never rejected business. Indeed, Frank Green had characterised himself as 'the industrious apprentice who slaved in the muck and grime so that the rest of the family could enjoy their lives of leisure.'[10] As I noted above, very few entrepreneurs retired from business entirely, perhaps out of a fear of surrendering influence and acceptance in one sphere to possible impotence and rejection in another. Even when large houses in the country were bought, favoured sons allowed to lead a life of luxury, or daughters married off to the sons of county families, the links with business and the wealth it bestowed were too strongly forged to be broken. Thus, some family businesses carried on through three generations, and most towns can provide several such examples – the Greens of Wakefield, the Fosters of Queensbury, the Cravens of Keighley, the Tetleys of Leeds, the Mitchells of Bradford, the Holdsworths of Halifax, the Croslands of Huddersfield, the Brooks of Meltham Mills. The family that turned its back on business to cultivate a gentle lifestyle was extremely uncommon.

John Dearman Birchall and James Kitson jnr of Leeds provide good examples of how easy it is to misinterpret the plutocratic household and its landed ambitions. Kitson, ironfounder and locomotive builder, had bought the Gledhow Hall estate near Leeds. The house had been built in the eighteenth century for the Leeds merchant Jeremiah Dixon, and, despite its rural position, had always been associated with trade. Kitson was an important figure in Leeds and was Liberal MP for the Colne Valley. At Gledhow he kept a household of around ten indoor servants and entertained on a mighty scale: his guests included political colleagues and even prime ministers. Yet Gledhow Hall could in no way be considered a country house. Its position on the edge of Leeds, for instance, suggests a good house with convenient access to business, rather than serious investment in a country estate. When Kitson died in 1911, he was worth £1,126,000 – cash and assets acquired mainly from industrial endeavour, not landed income.

Dearman Birchall, on the other hand, moved right out of the county when he bought Bowden Hall near Gloucester in 1868. Birchall had been born into a Quaker wool merchant family in Leeds, where he carried on the business as the partnership of J.D. Birchall & Company. If he was less active in the company's affairs after he had moved to Gloucestershire, he did not completely retire until he terminated his partnership in 1891, only six years before his death in 1897. For much of the intervening period he had made frequent railway journeys to Leeds on both social and business errands.[11]

The point about these two cases is that neither James Kitson, nor Dearman Birchall could have supported their ways of life on the income from their estates. While Kitson might appear the Liberal grandee with a place in the country, in truth he possessed only 150 acres. And while Dearman Birchall might play the country squire, his estate was not listed in Bateman's survey, despite having a 500-acre farm. In other words, their primary source of income was business. These conclusions are broadly in line with Rubinstein's where he proposes that few businessmen gave up their businesses entirely; and it aligns with Trainor's study of Black Country elites in the nineteenth century which he found contained a diversity of families with few seeking the country life and the majority retaining urban and industrial influence. Recent studies have revealed similar developments in parts of Europe. Smeets' study of the Twente district of the Netherlands suggests that while nineteenth-century industrialists bought land and developed these estates, yet, by and large, they did not mix in the same social circles as traditional landed elites, and seem to have regarded their estates more as a mark of their success and standing as industrialists rather than an attempt at an entré into aristocratic society.[12]

This last line of argument bears out the point that many entrepreneurs seem to have viewed their homes as a fitting symbol of their superior social position and as an opportunity for self-aggrandisement. This could take different forms. There was the power architecture of the house itself – Meanwood Towers, Milner Field, Cliffe Castle or Whinburn were huge and costly mansions bristling with ornamentation or having a bastion-like, architectonic quality. Other houses might have an imposing entrance with

The entrance to Foxhill. Tetley's monogram and the date 1863 appear in the somewhat weathered arabesque frieze above the door, while to either side of the arch are crests set, to the left, in vine leaves and, to the right, among hops.

The hall fireplace at Banney Royd.

a tower above or a carriage porch. At Foxhill, Weetwood, George Corson designed a great defensive tower as the entrance to the Tetley house, embellishing its pointed arched doorway with his client's crest and motto.

Houses such as the above are in some ways the exception, for perhaps the majority of the houses built by newly rich families were notable, not for their extravagant proportions, but for their moderate size considering the wealth of their builders. It was inside, however, that wealth was often on display, and the opulent interiors of these houses remain impressive. Here, crests, mottoes and epigrams of all sorts became much-used decorative devices: an awe-inspiring decorative treatment incorporating a high-sounding maxim might speak the wealth and sagacity of its owner. Such devices might also be used to proclaim a due respect for the virtues of domesticity and fly the pennant of an elite who saw themselves as the guardians of respectability, at home, to use Mark Girouard's term, in the moral house.[13] Thus, on entering the hall at Lady Royd Hall, Bradford, one is struck by the richness of the interior and the huge hall fireplace with the words 'Charity thinketh no evil' carved in gothic script across its stone canopy. On retiring at Foxhill, the guest was left in no doubt about the salubrity of regular hours, for carved into the capitals of columns supporting an arcade around the bed chamber landing are a series of maxims such as 'The foster nurse of nature is repose', while at Banney Royd the domestic virtues are extolled in the somewhat gnomic line, 'Each Man's Chimney Is His Golden Milestone', written above the hall fireplace.

Monograms were a particularly popular way of stamping one's mark on a place, and can be found at many houses worked in variety of materials. Monograms and initials can

Edward Beaumont used the elephant and castle crest on the faces of the entrance tower at his house Stoneleigh, Huddersfield; a symbol, perhaps, of business sagacity and perseverance.

be found in relief on the exterior of Joseph Barker's Holmefield at Thornes, or T.R. Harding's St Anne's Tower at Burley, near Leeds, or Sir Mark Oldroyd's Hyrstlands at Batley. Internally they are carved into the woodwork of the library at Lady Royd Hall, or the staircase at Oak Bank House, Keighley; carved into the marble keystones of fireplaces at Bowling Park [D], Bradford, or Bankfield, Halifax; etched into glass at Malsis Hall, Sutton-in-Craven, and in stained glass at Crow Nest, Dewsbury. The apotheosis of this self-aggrandisement occurs at Cliffe Castle, Keighley. Here the Butterfield crest can be found in several places and the Butterfield monogram has been used all over the hall and vestibule as a decorative motif. The mezzanine window lighting the staircase depicts in stained and leaded glass the Butterfield family in Elizabethan dress flanked by portraits of royalty. Butterfield's pride in his own house and the success such houses reflected is clearly expressed in a letter to his son in 1878:

> Yesterday I called on the Holdens and found his mansion superbly furnished and organised, but the rockery and other things required yet a year's work to finish, and after all, I much prefer Cliffe Castle. From there we drove over to Mr Lund's [i.e. Malsis Hall] and I found him at home, and his house doubled in size and beauty, indeed Cliffe, Oakworth and his are far ahead of any neighbouring residences.[14]

It is interesting that this sort of personal advertisement rarely occurs in earlier Classical houses. It is as if entrepreneurial families developed a new awareness of their social

Above: The monogram of Henry and Mary Illingworth above the library door at Lady Royd Hall, Bradford.

Left: At Whinburn, Keighley, the initials of Prince Smith appear in several places both inside and outside the house in a variety of materials. Here they are worked into the lead hopper of a fall pipe.

Opposite: The Butterfield family in their glory at Cliffe Castle, Keighley.

position after the 1850s. If W.J. Fox, a Unitarian minister and social commentator, could write in 1835 of 'an almost universal unfixedness of position' among the middle class, with everyone 'rising or falling'[15], this was not the case among the newly rich families of West Yorkshire after 1850. While there were falls from grace and bankruptcies, the established new rich did not suffer the financial panics and disasters of the first risky decades of the nineteenth century. They tended to remain an economically stable and wealthy group on the whole. The period 1850-1875, moreover, if not quite the boom years described by some historians,[16] was, nevertheless, a period of prosperity for many including Yorkshire manufacturers. It is no coincidence that the majority of the houses in this study, where dates of erection can be ascertained, were built then. The graph[17] below shows this quite clearly, indicating the prosperity and confidence of the middle class in these years.

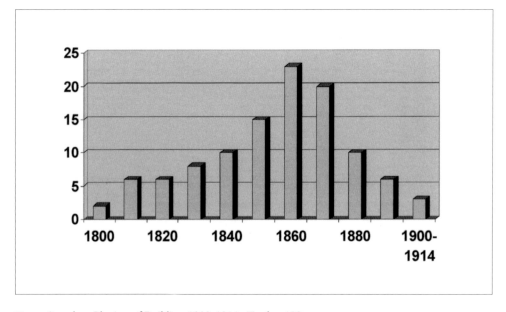

House Sample – Phasing of Building 1800-1914. Total = 109.

While a minority of new rich may have remained stubbornly true to their origins, and while a minority of others may have pursued a country estate and a life of gentility, the majority seem to have sought something different. They had achieved great wealth; they were talented businessmen, some household names; they recognised that they held an increasingly important position in society. A good house and garden, a country place for relaxation, even the possibility of a knighthood or baronetcy – all were very acceptable, and all were a well-earned mark of their achievements and their position, but it was a position in which they were able to stand on their own two feet. If some few thought it desirable to emulate the nobility and gentry, then they might; and if they wished, they might also buy up small gentry estates when they came onto the market, as some did. Yet the majority probably felt no need for this, realising that they were, in a sense, the equals or counterparts of landowning families: an urban industrial elite, rather than a traditional landed elite.

The position is thrown into sharp relief by Sir Titus Salt's remarks. Salt had made his fortune from a large spinning and manufacturing business in Bradford, pioneering the use of Alpaca yarns and the production of lustre cloths. As a socially concerned industrialist he cherished the notion of building a model mill and industrial village far removed from the smoke and grime of Bradford. Accordingly, between 1850 and 1870 he laid out around £250,000 in the building of his village, Saltaire, in a rural position on the banks of the River Aire at Shipley. Salt himself was a well-respected figure who had been elected MP for Bradford and who was on friendly terms with the leading county families such as the Earl of Harewood and the Earl of Mexborough. In 1853 Salt was fifty, and in the same year the first building in his model industrial village, the mill, was completed. Harewood was invited to the opening ceremony, and enquired of Salt why, at the age of fifty, he was entering on a vast new business venture when he might retire to some pleasant country estate to enjoy his great fortune. Salt replied:

> My Lord, I had made up my mind to do this very thing, but on reflection I determined otherwise. In the first place I thought that by the concentration of my works in one locality I might provide occupation for my sons. Moreover, as a landed proprietor I felt I should be out of my element. You are a nobleman with all the influence that rank and large estates can bring. Consequently you have power and influence in the country. But outside of my business I am nothing. In it, I have considerable influence. By the opening of Saltaire, I also hope to do good to my fellow men.[18]

TEN CASE HISTORIES

1. ARMLEY HOUSE, LEEDS

Armley House was designed for Benjamin Gott around 1816 by Sir Robert Smirke, a leading Greek Revival architect of the early nineteenth century. Gott was born into a tradesman/professional family at Woodhall near Calverley in 1762. After an education at Bingley Grammar School, Benjamin was apprenticed to Wormald & Fountaine a firm of Leeds cloth merchants. He prospered in this business, and was the motivating force behind the building of Bean Ing Mills in 1792. By 1816 he had taken over the entire enterprise and was trading as Benjamin Gott & Sons. Bean Ing was the first really large woollen mill where most of the production processes were grouped together on one site with steam supplying the motive power. By 1800, 1,000 people were employed, and the mill was regarded as a wonder, attracting visitors from both England and abroad. At the same time, Gott extended the mercantile branch of the business to export markets in Europe, America and the East.

All this made Gott an extremely wealthy man. In 1804, he had bought an estate at Armley with a small Classical house of the previous century. In 1809, he commissioned the most celebrated landscape gardener then living, Humphry Repton, to redesign both house and garden. Although much of Repton's advice on the garden was followed, his design for the house was rejected in favour of one by Smirke[1]. Smirke seems to have followed the basic outine of Repton's design, but recast it, not as a pretty villa as Repton had it, but as a monumental neo-classical house. The original house was retained centrally, but given a pediment supported on giant Ionic columns, and two severely detailed wings were added at either end[2], work that seems to have been carried out between 1816 and 1817. Internally, Smirke seems to have accepted much of Repton's planning, and with it Repton's idea that the central room should be lined with mirrors to reflect the terrace and garden. In 1835, John Sawrey Gilpin, another eminent landscape designer, carried out further work on the gardens, and at some point a flight of steps with balustrades was added to the terrace.

This was the house in which Gott entertained fashionable visitors to the mill; in which he displayed his collection of paintings and sculpture; and where, according to Repton, there should be 'clocks, and bronzes, and cut glass, and China, and Library-tables, covered with books, and pamphlets, and reviews, and newspapers; which contribute to the elegant and rational enjoyment of modern life.'[3]

Gott died in 1840, declaring an estate of £200,000 – contemporaries reckoned his worth to be above £1 million. Considering his lifestyle, enormous income and the scale of his undertakings, this could well have been correct.

The house is today owned by Leeds Council. The grounds are a municipal golf course; the house, its wings demolished and in a ramshackle condition, is the club house.

Above and below: Armley House.

Clifton House.

2. CLIFTON HOUSE, BRADFORD

It was not at all unusual in the nineteenth century to find numbers of Germans living in England, particularly in the textile districts of the North. Bradford was no exception, and a brisk trade was conducted there in cloth and yarn. Many firms set up export houses in the town, one quarter earning the name Little Germany, while *The Voice of the People*, a local radical newspaper, rudely stated in one edition that the Bradford streets stank of cigars and Germans.

It is difficult to ascertain the exact wealth of many of these merchants, since they retained property in Germany, and probably some of their profits found their way back home, also. Other Germans became naturalised British subjects, building houses and settling down in Bradford. One such was Jacob Philipp. Born in Hamburg in 1817, he came to Bradford in 1841, becoming a partner in the export house of N.P. & H. Nathan. In 1864, he established his own export business, J. Philipp & Company with a warehouse in Vicar Lane.

He was already a man of some substance. In 1851, he had commissioned the Bradford architects Andrews & Delauney to design a house for him in Manningham, the best of the Bradford suburbs. This was Clifton House, a large Classical villa. It has an impressive Tuscan portico spanning the recessed central entrance. In 1863, the house was extended with a billiard room linked to the main house by a conservatory. Internally, the rooms are arranged in a near symmetrical villa plan.[4]

Clifton House is interesting in another respect, also. It shows how, despite the pleas of architectural purists for designs in one great style, and that a Gothic style, architects, nevertheless, continued to design in a variety of styles to suit the demands of their clients. Andrews & Delauney came up with a Classical design for Clifton House, yet Philipp's neighbour chose an Elizabethan style for Rosemount House designed by the same firm two or three years earlier.

Philipp resided at Clifton House until his death in 1897. The family lived in some luxury with six servants at one point, although with only a small garden and no stables or carriage house. A row of ledges supported on cantilevers down the west side of the house are probably the remains of window box mounts – cast-iron rails to retain the boxes appear to have been removed. This is a villa on a suburban site, reflecting, perhaps, Philipp's lesser wealth – he left an estate valued at £47,000 – but good testimony to the relative exclusiveness of even lesser wealth and the high quality of architecture it could command.

3. RAVENSKNOWLE, HUDDERSFIELD

John Beaumont of Dalton, near Huddersfield, is one of the more interesting textile barons, because he made his money from both manufacturing and designing. Indeed, in 1875, he was appointed head of textile design at the Yorkshire College, the forerunner of Leeds University. Beaumont was born in 1820 at Dalton, the son of a fancy woollen weaver. He showed an early talent for the design of fancy, and was to become the consultant to several Huddersfield firms, eventually entering into a partnership with the Tolsons of Dalton who were to win a gold medal at the Great Exhibition of 1851 for their fancy woollens. After a spell designing tweeds for a Scottish company, he returned to Huddersfield where, just before retiring from manufacturing, he inaugurated the weaving of fancy worsteds around 1870. He was said to have also made successful investments in railways and became chairman of the North British Railway.

Opposite and above: Ravensknowle.

In the 1850s, he began the construction of a large house just to the east of Huddersfield. The architect Beaumont chose was a London man, Richard Tress, of the firm of Tress & Chambers. The house was built in a palatial Italian style whose design origins probably lie in the renaissance palaces of Rome. At first sight, there are similarities with Clifton House, the previous case history, especially in the use of a recessed central entrance. But what differentiates Italianate houses of this kind from late neo-classical designs like Clifton House, is a more ornamental approach – the use of arcaded windows and florid decoration, for example, the latter amply demonstrated by the bay window to the morning room. The compound shaping of the arched heads to this window requires a high degree of skill from the mason: not only do they have to arch vertically, but they also have to curve horizontally to correspond to the radius of the window's arc. Another prominent feature is the loggia above the main entrance. Only one other house in the county – Hayfield House at Glusburn – seems to have had a first-floor loggia like this. Perhaps there were good reasons – it would have provided a cool and shady place to sit in Florence or Rome, but in Huddersfield?

Through the main entrance is an octagonal marble-floored vestibule with cloakrooms off. The hub of the house is a top-lit saloon from which the day rooms open, and which gave access to a conservatory, now demolished. Beaumont also employed the latest in security devices – metal blinds or shutters that slid into position across the windows when a mechanism inside the house was operated.

It was fittings like these that added to the cost of building: the final bill is thought to have amounted to getting on for £20,000. Beaumont could afford it. He died in 1889 leaving his daughter Sarah Martha an estate worth £520,200. Under her married name of Mrs Grove-Grady she was one of the wealthiest women in the country in her own right. She eventually sold Ravensknowle to a relative – Legh Tolson – preferring to live at her house in Ilkley or at her London home.

4. HEADINGLEY CASTLE, LEEDS

There are some houses that one comes across where only the vaguest of details about architect and owner are available, yet the house is of a quality that cannot be ignored. Headingley Castle falls into this category.

By the middle of the nineteenth century there was a movement west out of Leeds by its wealthier families to the rural village of Headingley, which soon developed into an exclusive suburb. John Marshall, the Leeds flax spinner, had bought land there, and in 1837 he leased some to Thomas England, a corn merchant also of Leeds. A deed of 1843 relates that England now had a dwelling house 'in the course of being erected on part of the said Lands'. This house was Headingley Castle, originally called The Elms. The grounds seem to have consisted of an old quarry and several closes, but field boundaries were removed and a small, undulating landscape was created as the setting for the new house.

The architect was John Child. The design is transitional between the Gothic of the eighteenth century and the Gothic Revival of the Victorian period. Its style is Tudor or Elizabethan, although its form owes a great deal to the symmetrical Classical villa, and the ground plan is based on villa planning with the rooms grouped evenly around a central hall. Several houses were built in this way: that is, as boxes, almost, that could be given Classical or Gothic details, according to the client's fancy. But where Headingley Castle scores higher than most is in its Gothic interior, a finely judged balance in which decorative detail is applied with a lightness of touch often lacking in some later interiors.

Headingley Castle.

Headingley Castle.

During the 1840s and 1850s, houses in well-developed revived Elizabethan styles were built in several parts of the region, often with curvilinear gables and more subtle, asymmetrical massing than Headingley Castle. But one feature which the house perhaps introduced into the area can be found in its tower-like entrance with oriel window and castellated top, a feature possibly copied from one of the many pattern books available. Here, the tower has a carriage porch with Tudor arches for good measure.

Little is known about England himself, other than that he was a corn merchant and had made several speculations in land. He was evidently a man of means, living in style at Headingley with a large household staffed by seven indoor servants and a coachman and gardener who were quartered in the stable yard. But here the mystery begins, for he seems either to have moved away from Headingley in the later 1860s, or died. All local references to him disappear after 1868. More puzzling still, is that no grant of probate or administration of his estate was entered in the probate calendar, the official record, for the whole of the nineteenth century.

5. BANKFIELD, HALIFAX

Of all the houses in these case histories. Bankfield has undergone the most complicated development. It seems to have started life as the villa of Thomas Greenwood, a Halifax cotton and worsted spinner. Greenwood had built Bankfield by about 1810, situated amid elevated rural surroundings in Northowram, well away from the growing industrialisation of Halifax, a place that Anne Lister of Shibden Hall was to describe in 1837 as a 'large smoke-canopied commercial town'.[5] At around this time, the Greenwood family sold Bankfield. The buyer was Jonathan Akroyd and his son Edward, partners in one of the most successful worsted firms of the Halifax district.

Jonathan, who had also acquired land nearby at Haley Hill, built himself a new house, Woodside, close by the factory he had established there – Haley Hill Shed. Edward, then twenty-eight and recently married, seems to have been content for a while with Greenwood's old house, which can still be seen, though enmeshed in later extensions. From what remains this appears to have been a fairly modest double pile plan house, but with a degree of pretension in its neo-classical detailing and somewhat Egyptian-looking broadly coved eaves. However, between 1840 and 1850 Edward Akroyd began to extend the house, adding single-storey glazed galleries to the ground floor and building out a new dining room to the south shown in the print of about 1866. He also included a small domestic chapel, a rare development in houses of the new rich.

Jonathan Akroyd died in 1847. As the century progressed, his son Edward became an increasingly important figure in Halifax. Not only was he the employer of large numbers of people, but he also constructed a model village, Akroyden, near his house; he had contributed liberally to the erection of public buildings and churches, and he was returned as a Liberal MP for Halifax. Perhaps feeling the need for a house commensurate with his status, in 1867 he again enlarged Bankfield. This was the most important stage of the building for which he engaged the Atkinson brothers of York as his architects.[6] They added a grand block to the north containing a new arrangement of day rooms, unusually planned on two levels. Entrance is into a marble-lined vestibule with billiard room and smoking room to one side. A flight of stairs leads the visitor past Roman-style murals

Bankfield.

Above and below: Bankfield.

and up to a first-floor saloon from which further day rooms open. The new block tied together the old house and Akroyd's earlier, straggling additions, converting the whole into a unique palazzo-style house. But while the earlier work is Classical, the Atkinsons' block has a North Italian Gothic air with its tracery windows and fanned arches; the capitals of some columns look decidedly Venetian. At the same time, decorative motifs from the earlier work appear to have been copied and reinterpreted on the new.[7]

Edward Akroyd died twenty years later in 1887, having changed from a Methodist to an Anglican, from a Liberal to a Conservative, and having withdrawn further and further from business. His will was proved at £1,200, much of his money being spent on building and political and social interests. Even so, this is a paltry amount compared with the £300,000 left by his father.

6. MEANWOOD TOWERS, LEEDS

Thomas Stuart Kennedy was of Scottish extraction. He was cousin to Sir Andrew Fairbairn, the Leeds textile machine maker, whose firm Kennedy entered, eventually to become a partner. Fairbairns were perhaps the most successful textile engineers in Leeds, and after a relatively short business career Kennedy retired from the firm in 1882 at the early age of forty-three. He took up residence at his country home, Park Hill, near Wetherby, where he devoted himself to field sports. He was a surprisingly energetic man and a keen mountaineer, being a member of the Alpine Club and joining a climbing expedition to the Himalayas. He died in 1894, leaving £80,578, a surprisingly small estate when compared with the other partners in Fairbairns.

On his profits as a partner Kennedy was able to commission E. W. Pugin, son of the more famous A. W. N. Pugin, to design a house for him at Meanwood in 1867. Originally

Meanwood
Towers.

Meanwood Towers.

known as Meanwood House, this was a large and extravagantly detailed piece of Gothic architecture, built of rubble walling with Coade Stone dressings. The architectural historian Derek Linstrum aptly summed up the house as 'using ornamental chimney stacks and oriel windows in abandoned profusion,' a description not far removed from the opinions of some architectural commentators of the day, for while one thought 'the work deserving of careful study', he qualified this statement by adding that 'the tall stone chimneys ... conflict to some degree with the pretensions of the tower, and the excessive use of gargoyles is such as few but those imbued with medieval ardour would now be led to indulge in.'[8] The interior seems to have been freely planned around a central hall and gallery, a conservatory opened from the dining room and there was a tower room from which good views of the surrounding district could be enjoyed. Kennedy's collection of paintings had been on show in the house, and he had commissioned Schulze & Sons of Germany to build an organ which was situated in an organ house in the grounds.

One tantalising question is posed by a 1920 sale catalogue of the house.[9] This states that Richard Norman Shaw also had a hand in the design. The detailing of the exterior is so unlike Shaw's work that one feels inclined to dismiss the suggestion, but the *British Architect* article quoted above confirms this. The original termination to the tower had been a spire, but Shaw rebuilt it as a part-timbered and gabled structure reminiscent of some of his gatehouses.

During the course of the twentieth century, Meanwood Towers has suffered a number of assaults on its fabric – most of the chimneys have been shortened and the tower truncated. It is now subdivided into flats, and its gardens are built over with modern houses. Yet it is still a striking sight, and one comes across it like a great, beached wreck.

7. HOLMEFIELD HOUSE, WAKEFIELD

Wakefield did not undergo quite the industrialisation that Leeds and Bradford experienced, but it did have its share, and a number of industrial dynasties held sway in and around the town. The Greens (ironfounders), the Holdsworths (dyers), the Marriotts and Barkers (worsted) would head any such list of families. The Barker family's origins are somewhat obscure. Robert Henry Barker was born at the end of the eighteenth century, and how he spent his early years is uncertain, although he may have learned something of the worsted trade working for the Marriotts. By the 1830s, he had begun a spinning business in Wakefield as the partnership of Barker & Poppleton, and in the nearby village of Thornes he occupied Thornes Mill as the firm of R.H. Barker & Company. He seems to have lived at the mill house there, and his mother and younger brother, Joseph, lived nearby. However, Joseph moved to Westfield Villa, a small house at Horbury, in the 1840s. By the 1850s, Robert was perhaps in semi-retirement and had exchanged places with Joseph at Westfield Villa. Later he moved to Hall Croft, a Georgian house, also at Horbury, where he died in 1857 leaving an estate of £10,000.

When Holmefield House, along the road from Thornes Mill, came up for sale at the end of the 1850s, Joseph Barker was the buyer. Holmefield had been built in the 1830s, but it is uncertain just what form this house took, since Barker commissioned the Bradford firm of Lockwood & Mawson[10] to rebuild it in 1864. This was a thorough remodelling in a Gothic style, leaving little of the original house untouched. In 1875, Holmefield was again remodelled by heightening Lockwood & Mawson's single-storey billiard room and by extensions at the south end, and the interior had been fitted up by the Leeds firm, Marsh & Jones. In its completed form it contained a drawing room, library,

Above and below: Holmefield.

dining room and billiard room opening off a transverse corridor, together with service rooms. To minister to his needs, Barker had an indoor staff of seven servants including a butler and a footman.

Despite spending what must have been a large sum of money on the house and engaging leading architects and craftsmen, Holmefield fails to excite. Although the entrance front shows promise, it, nevertheless, suffers from the same faults as the garden front in its thin and unimaginative detailing which is poorly integrated into the design. There is also a clumsy disjunction of roofs, the result of two remodellings. Barker's initials and the date 1875 are carved into the two shields below the strip of moulding on the left-hand gable – detail which appears curiously disembodied.

In some respects the Barkers are more typical of many newly rich families and their houses: that is, they sometimes preferred to buy existing houses rather than build new ones, or they put up with insipid designs which lacked the sophistication shown by several houses in these case histories.

Joseph Barker died in 1892, well-respected among his workpeople, many of whom lined his funeral route. He left an estate worth £300,600.

8. THE ICKRINGILLS' HOUSES AT KEIGHLEY

Case histories 8 and 9 show the range of houses that families at opposite ends of the wealth scale could produce in the same town. All are situated in Keighley, a place we think of today as a perhaps a typical Aire Valley town – a 1960s shopping centre surrounded by municipal buildings and older shops with factories on the outskirts of town. In the nineteenth century, however, Keighley was heavily industrialised, possessing something like 10% of all the worsted mills in the country, and several large manufacturing fortunes were made, yet Keighley retained a small-town feel.

Ira and James Ickringill were somewhat unusual entrepreneurs. They were one of the few examples of a working class family making it to the big time. Their father had been an overlooker in a mill, and they had begun their lives as mill operatives. From such beginnings they went on to establish a worsted spinning business that became one of the largest in the region by the beginning of the twentieth century, with premises at both Keighley and Bradford.

In 1885 Ira had put some of his profits into building a fine house, Laurel Mount, which was located to the north of the town where some of the best houses were to be found. It was designed by the firm of W.H. & A. Sugden a Keighley partnership of some flair. They produced at Laurel Mount a stylish Queen Anne house, and although somewhat mannered – notice the different pediments to the windows in the gables, for example – this is a minor criticism. Overall the house is a gem: small, but delightfully detailed, especially inside with the use of oak panelling and blue- and white-tiled fireplaces. The mezzanine window that lights the stairs contains two female figures in coloured glass representing painting and sculpture.

The houses that James built are a contrast in every way. They occupied a site in an unfashionable part of the town off Oakworth Road, they were near the mill and the land separating house and mill he filled with back-to-back houses for his workforce. James had lived in an older house at Holy Croft, Oakworth Road, for several years when in 1898 he submitted a plan for another house there. One wonders what his architects, the Sugdens, thought of his demands. The ground floor was to contain two sitting rooms, a bedroom and a kitchen. Although James obtained planning consent, the house was never

Laurel Mount.

Balcony House.

built. James did build another house there in 1903, although he never lived in it. Instead he eventually took up residence at Balcony House. This was built in 1908 across from the 1903 house. The architect is unknown, but it may again have been the Sugdens. It is the oddest house built in the county – small, meanly detailed and with a timber balcony that gives it more the air of a tenement than the house of a wealthy man. The site is now empty and dilapidated.

Ira died in 1911 leaving an unusually small estate valued at only £26,000. James died in 1924 leaving an estate of £89,000.

9. WHINBURN, KEIGHLEY

William Smith of Keighley was a clock maker who began a textile machinery making business, taking his five sons into partnership. He died in 1850, although the firm continued under his sons until 1865 when the partnership was dissolved. One of his sons, Prince Smith I, founded his own machine making business, taking *his* son, Prince Smith II, into partnership. Prince Smith II built the business into a most important concern, which, by the beginning of the twentieth century, under the management of Prince Smith II and his son (inevitably) Prince Smith III, became the largest textile machinery making firm in Europe, if not the world.

Whinburn was built for Prince Smith III (who later changed his name to Prince Prince-Smith). It is situated just to the north of Keighley on a steep site overlooking the Aire Valley. Two stages of building occurred. The first was to the designs of James Ledingham, a talented Scottish architect practicing in Bradford. Ledingham's design of 1897 was for a large, but comfortable house in the sort of vernacular manor house style popular at the time. However, Prince Smith does not seem to have been satisfied with it and in 1912 he commissioned the London firm of Simpson & Ayrton to enlarge the house which they did during 1912 and 1913. Their work consisted of creating an immense baronial hall with a large inglenook and screens passage, adding a servants' hall and building the north end of the house into a tower.[11] Some of Ledingham's work had a domestic charm, but the additions made to the front by Simpson & Ayrton give the house a bastion-like quality, with parts built almost as if for defence. Internally and externally the craftsmanship is superb – panelling, domestic fixtures and fittings and metalwork are all of the best quality, whether prominently on display, or in inferior positions. This concern with design extends all round the house and to the rear – no Queen Anne front/Mary Anne back, here.

Both Prince Smiths I and II occupied houses in suburban settings in Spring Gardens Lane, Keighley, at Holly House and Hillbrook respectively. These are modest villas, taking into account the family wealth – Prince Smith II left above £1 million. They were, perhaps, the family's town houses, for they owned another house in the village of Southburn, near Great Driffield. In Whinburn, however, we see the peak of their house-building activities. It is a powerful statement of their wealth and importance, and there is possibly an element of rivalry with Cliffe Castle, the greatly extended Butterfield mansion about half a mile down the road.

Whinburn is now empty and owned by Bradford Council. It is a house and garden that ought to be better known. The garden, indeed, is one of the most important Arts and Crafts-influenced gardens in the North of England, possibly designed by Thomas H. Mawson, and yet it is falling badly into disrepair.

Above and opposite: Whinburn.

Left and below: Heathcote

10. HEATHCOTE, ILKLEY

One approaches Heathcote with some trepidation: an important house which cannot be ignored, but one that has received a good deal of attention from architectural writers. The record does need to be set straight, however, on one point. The house was not built for *Ernest* Hemingway, but for *John Thomas* Hemingway. It seems to have been Christopher Hussey who perpetrated this mistake, confusing him, no doubt, with the American novelist, but the mistake has been repeated ever since. J.T. Hemingway was born in humble circumstances at Shelf, near Halifax. His early years are obscure, but he became an employee of the Bradford wool merchants, Richardsons. He eventually became manager there, then, in 1896, a partner; by 1906, he was sole partner and owner of this important export house.

What made Hemingway light on Lutyens as architect for his new house in 1906 is unknown. Also, it is clear from Lutyens's letters that he regarded the Hemingways as ungracious arrivees. Be that as it may, Lutyens accepted the commission to design the house at Ilkley. What he did not want to design was the sort of Gothic or Vernacular Revival manor house that he saw around him there – 'The other villas have a window from this, a door from that etc. – a pot-pourri of Yorkeological detail.' What Hemingway got instead was a grand Classical villa with an almost sculptural quality to its exterior detailing and a remarkably soft colour contrast between the red tiles of the roof and the ochre walls. This is brought about by an expert knowledge and a subtle use of materials – the common walling is Guiseley grit, but the ground-floor walls and dressings are Morley stone, a little-used stone that tends to exude iron salts, bleeding to a rusty yellow ochre.

There are several good descriptions of the house already[12] and there seems little point in adding another, but two things are worth emphasising. Only Linstrum has remarked on Lutyens's debt to James Paine, the eighteenth-century architect who completed several works in the county. A distinctive feature of some of Paine's houses is the massing – a tall central block flanked by shorter pavilions to produce a triangular grouping. Stockeld Park, New Grange, Kirkstall, or St Ives [D], Bingley, are local examples of this. So is Heathcote – 'I have been scolded for not being Yorkshire in Yorkshire', wrote Lutyens.[13] Yet, it is perhaps characteristic of the man that his architectural allusions were to Yorkshire's classical traditions, rather than to its more obvious Jacobean manor houses.

There are also a number of other small allusions at Heathcote, easily missed, if Hemingway is ignored or misrepresented. As an export merchant, for example, he had travelled widely and had developed trade with the Far East. Reference is made to this in the cartouches above the ground-floor windows, the ship being a symbol of overseas trade.

Hemingway died in 1926, leaving an estate valued at £306,500, but he possessed undisclosed property in the East. Lutyens had recorded that Hemingway was far better-off than he seemed, and his true worth was perhaps nearer £500,000.

GAZETTEER OF
SURVIVING HOUSES

This is a list of surviving entrepreneurs' houses which were recorded for the study. Where dates of building and names of architects are followed by a question mark, this indicates a conjecture. Unless otherwise stated, all the following houses are private and there is no right of public access.

Readers should understand that this is not an exhaustive list, and that some of the houses on it are of no great architectural merit. They were recorded to reflect the range of houses constructed.

To gain a better understanding of this range, I recommend a stroll around places such as Headingley, near Leeds, Manningham, near Bradford, or the Edgerton and Birkby districts of Huddersfield. Here numbers of houses, clearly visible from the road, are clustered together in what were once select suburbs. Heaton and Low Baildon to the north of Bradford also contain numbers of good-quality Arts and Crafts-influenced houses.

Adel Willows, Adel: vernacular-looking Gothic house, rubble built in long double pile range with service wing to rear. Built probably late 1850s or early 1860s for the Schunck family, German yarn and stuff merchants. An unprepossessing house given the wealth and standing of the Schuncks.

Airville, Shipley: small suburban villa typical of many in the Bradford area. Designed in French Classical style by Samuel Jackson, 1866, for Joseph Wade, Bradford worsted spinner. Much original work survives, but after a complete internal remodelling.

Armitage Bridge House, Honley: small Classical house said to have been built in 1828 for John Brooke of Armitage Bridge Mills, woollen manufacturer. Originally stood in landscaped garden.

Armley House, Leeds: rebuilding of small eighteenth-century house 1816-17 as grand neo-classical mansion by Robert Smirke for Benjamin Gott, merchant and woollen manufacturer of Leeds. Gardens remodelled by Repton and William Sawrey Gilpin. Public access to municipal golf course around house

Arncliffe, Headingley, Leeds: small brick house on a suburban site built in 1893 to half-butterfly plan. Francis Bedford for J.E. Bedford, manufacturing chemist. Pretty Queen Anne garden house also survives with painted glass rounds by G.F. Malins.

Balcony House, Keighley: small house built at beginning of twentieth century for James Ickringill, worsted spinner, possibly by W.H. & A. Sugden. Most unusual house with timber balcony to first floor. Derelict at time of writing.

Bankfield, Cottingley: large Elizabethan-style house designed by Andrews & Delauney in 1848 for William Murgatroyd, worsted spinner of Bradford. Later enlarged by same practice for Henry Mason, another Bradford worsted man.

Bankfield, Halifax: originally modest villa, but transformed into Gothic palazzo by Atkinsons of York *c.* 1867 for Edward Akroyd, worsted spinner and manufacturer. Pompeian-style frescoes to marble-lined staircase in vestibule, and painted library ceiling with rounds containing portraits of Chaucer, Shakespeare, Milton and Tennyson. Museum – public access to house and grounds.

Banney Royd, Birkby, Huddersfield: house designed by Edgar Wood and built 1902 for the accountant W.H. Armitage. Hybrid style – Manor House with Art Nouveaux tendencies. Extended with conservatory designed by Wood in 1904. This since truncated, spoiling Wood's careful balance of forms. Many original features survive, but not painted frieze in the hall by F.W. Jackson.

Bardon Grange, Weetwood, Leeds: Italianate house in pleasingly irregular grouping. Built for Bradford worsted merchant William Brown between 1859 and 1861 (communication from Jean K. Brown); Cuthbert Broderick?

Beeches The, Keighley: rebuilding of earlier house mostly in 1894 for worsted manufacturer J.H. Craven by John Haggas. Manor House style.

Belle Vue, Halifax: large Classical French villa with monumental interior designed by G.F. Stokes in 1857 for Sir Frank Crossley, carpet manufacturer. Well restored iron and glass conservatory attached to house, and Gothic belvedere in grounds which appear to have been the work of Milner & Paxton.

Belmont, Headingley, Leeds: villa built in Italianate style possibly for George Bray, gas engineer, and probably in 1870s.

Bermerside, Halifax: bland house built 1872 for Edward Crossley, carpet manufacturer, by Roger Ives. Chiefly remarkable for the observatory it once possessed – another of the Crossley boys' scientific pursuits.

Bowling House, Bowling, Bradford: small neo-classical house built within boundary of Bowling Ironworks for J.G. Paley, partner in company.

Briarcourt, Lindley, Huddersfield: house designed by Edgar Wood for cotton spinner and card maker John Sykes in 1894. Manor House Arts and Crafts in pleasingly irregular grouping. Superb internal detailing in Jacobean style. Painted frieze by Lancashire artist F.W. Jackson still survives, if in run-down state. Enlarged with billiard room, laundry and extra bedrooms in 1904 by Huddersfield architect W. Cooper.

Broadfold House, Luddenden: Classical French villa for John Murgatroyd jnr, worsted spinner and manufacturer. By 1877; architect possibly one of Dearden family.

Buckingham House, Headingley, Leeds: late neo-classical house built probably 1835–40 for James Hargreave woollen merchant. Garden front unadorned except for pediment and doric pilasters at angles. Billiard room (?) of single storey added slightly later. Internally remains of good plasterwork and decoration. A fine house once.

Buckstone Hall, Rawden: large castellated house built 1860s for Bradford worsted merchant and manufacturer William Dewhirst. Castellated towers designed probably to create prominent skyline above wooded landscape.

Burley Lawn, Burley-in-Wharfedale: house built for textile merchant William Brayshay. Long low elevation with asymmetrically arranged Italianate detail. 1860s?; Milnes & France?

Catherine House – see Upper Shibden Hall

Carleton Grange, nr Pontefract: house already present when estate bought by Thomas Tew, banker. Tew rebuilt this *c.* 1874 as an Elizabethan-style house with conservatory.

Carr Manor, Stonegate Lane, Leeds: rebuilding of earlier house (Carr House) in Manor House style, for Thomas Clifford Albutt, medical practitioner, by E.S. Prior in 1879, although not completed until 1881.

Chapel Allerton Hall, Gledhow Lane, Leeds: large brick house of seventeenth-century origins extended by Sir John Barran and resulting in blank façade with add-on Gothic porch. Once possessed fine gardens, though, with a grand promenade, but these have now been built over.

Cliffe Castle, Keighley: important house of complex origins. Originally built for lawyer Christopher Netherwood by architect George Webster of Kendal in 1830s. This house bought in 1840s by Butterfield family, worsted manufacturers and merchants, and rebuilt by Henry Isaac Butterfield in: 1) 1874–78 architect George Smith; 2) 1880–82 architect Wilson Bailey. Result: massive Elizabethan-style house with towers, yet French interiors and two winter gardens. Now sadly mutilated. Museum and park with public access.

Clifton House, Manningham, Bradford: substantial late neo-classical villa on suburban site. Built in 1851 for German merchant Jacob Philipp to designs of Andrews & Delauney.

Croft, The – see Weetwood Croft.

Crosland Lodge, Crosland Moor, Huddersfield: Greek Revival house, 1830–50? Probably for George Crosland, woollen manufacturer and banker. Badly mutilated during nineteenth century, and interior stripped in twentieth.

Crow Nest, Dewsbury: small eighteenth-century house acquired and largely rebuilt – wings, second floor and pediment added – by Hague and Cook families, woollen manufacturers and bankers, in nineteenth century. Now somewhat mutilated – wings demolished. Public access, park and museum.

Currerwood – see Steeton Manor.

Daisy Bank, Girlington, Bradford: perhaps Bradford's first Gothic Revival house. Designed in Elizabethan style in 1845 by Andrews & Delauney for the worsted merchant George Greenwood Tetley, but later the home of worsted spinner and MP Alfred Illingworth.

Dobroyd Castle, Todmorden: large castellated house completed in 1869 to designs of John Gibson for John Fielden jnr, cotton manufacturer. Monumental top-lit saloon – arcade with marble piers; inlays; panels in relief showing cotton manufacture. Gardens by Edward Kemp.

Durker Roods, Meltham Mills: house of uncertain origins. Eclectically French in style, of perhaps late 1870s or '80s, but still built to villa plan around central top-lit hall. Original builder perhaps Sharples Fisher, silk spinner of Huddersfield, but later acquired (or originally built?) by Charles Brook of Meltham Mills.

Eastwood House, Keighley: Greek Revival house of quality, said to have been built in 1819 for William Sugden, worsted spinner, but shown on Greenwood's map of 1817. Architect unknown, but possibly George Webster. Façade survives, but in poor and neglected condition internally. Now part of theatre and municipal leisure complex; public access.

Eller Close, Roundhay, Leeds: small neo-classical house of good quality. 1820s? Occupied by William Ledgard, woollen manufacturer, for much of nineteenth century.

Field Head, Lindley, Huddersfield: small house of 1820 with Tuscan portico and bay windows. Acquired by card maker James Nield Sykes and enlarged by him with Italianate wing to south and smoking/billiard room in 1873 by Bolton architect George Woodhouse.

Fox Hill, Meanwood, Leeds: large Gothic house built to designs of George Corson in 1863 for the brewer William Francis Tetley. Extended 1913, with new library by Sydney D. Kitson; tower or spire removed at same date. Badly mutilated when used as country club in 1950s/60s.

Gleddings, the, Skircoat, Halifax: house acquired by George Henry Smith, wire maker, and extended by him in revived neo-classical style throughout 1890s, but principally in 1894.

Harehills Grove, Harehills, Leeds: small, but pleasing neo-classical house of 1820s built for James Brown, woollen merchant, and possibly designed by John Clark. Fine segmental portico on composite order columns.

Hawkstone, Keighley: house designed in 1865 for textile magnate B.F. Marriner, probably by William Andrews of Bradford. Small Gothic frontage with imposing tower, but land falls away to provide further rooms below. Set on small but impressive crag with woodland. Marriner died in 1866, and never seems to have lived there. It became the home of William Marriner Brigg and his wife Sarah Jane.

Headingley Castle, Headingley, Leeds: beautiful early Gothic house in Tudor/Elizabethan style. Well-preserved Gothic interior. Built 1843-46 for Thomas England, corn merchant, to the design of John Child.

Heathcote, Ilkley: house designed by Edwin Lutyens in 1906 for J.T. Hemingway, wool merchant. Classical house with massing reminiscent of James Paine. House stands on terrace with balconettes overlooking garden, also by Lutyens – sweep of lawn with plantings in perimeter walls, two short canals by terrace, highly formal box-edged beds below. Two summer houses terminate vistas at either end of terrace.

Helme Hall, near Meltham: large Manor House design in ashlar carried out in 1887 for Edward Hildred Carlile, cotton thread manufacturer. Simple hall and crosswing form. Good standard of craftsmanship inside – painted glass in naturalistic patterns reminiscent of Malins.

Highlands, Scalebor Park, Burley-in-Wharfedale: Arts and Crafts-influenced house in Manor House style. Built 1896 for worsted spinner William Henry Mitchell.

Hillbrook, Spring Gardens Lane, Keighley: substantial yet plainly detailed Gothic house built for Prince Smith II; late 1860s? Some later work on gardens by Thomas Mawson.

Holly House, Spring Gardens Lane, Keighley: modest house with Italianate detail of perhaps 1850s, carefully converted to two dwellings later in century. For many years home of Prince Smith I, machine maker, and possibly built for him.

Holmefield, Thornes, Wakefield: original house built in 1830s for Foljambe family of Wakefield, but acquired by Joseph Barker, worsted spinner, and rebuilt 1864 to designs of Lockwood & Mawson; further remodellings *c.* 1875, with interiors by Marsh & Jones of Leeds. Gothic with French overtones. Conference centre and restaurant standing in park; public access.

Hyrstlands, Batley Carr, Batley: rebuilding of earlier house in Northern Renaissance design in 1891 for woollen manufacturer Sir Mark Oldroyd. Well preserved with original conservatory and remains of garden.

Knowle Hall, Ingrow, Keighley: small neo-classical house built of fine ashlar with semi-circular bay window. For John Greenwood, cotton and worsted spinner *c.* 1800.

Lady Royde Hall, Bradford: Gothic house with powerful entrance built 1866 for worsted spinner and manufacturer Henry Illingworth to designs of Milnes & France; extended *c.* 1880 with library. Sumptuous interior well-preserved.

Langley, Baildon: Italianate house of 1877 on lavish scale and with well-preserved interior. Front entrance tower truncated. Possibly built for William Wright, chemical manufacturer.

Laurel Mount, Keighley: small Queen Anne house built 1885-86 for Ira Ickringill, worsted spinner, to designs of W.H. & A. Sugden. Much of interior remains together with mezzanine window containing in painted glass panels representing Sculpture and Painting. Garden loggia also survives.

Lawn, The – see Burley Lawn.

Longlands, Haworth: large Jacobean-style house designed by J.B. Bailey in 1884 for the worsted spinner and manufacturer Edwin Merrall. Eccentric carriage porch of grotesque design. Excellent stairs window in painted glass by G.F. Malins. Now a youth hostel.

Longwood Hall, Castlefields, Bingley: asymmetrical rural Italianate house built *c.* 1867 to designs of Lockwood & Mawson for William Marshall Selwyn, a partner in Bowling Ironworks. Some extensions and alterations later in the century.

Malsis Hall, Sutton-in-Craven: large and important house, the country retreat of James Lund, worsted spinner and manufacturer of Keighley. The rebuilding of earlier house to designs of Samuel Jackson, completed *c.* 1862, but further work probably carried out until *c.* 1880. Italianate with French overtones; tower to north-east; some painted ceilings survive, including frieze in library with portraits of several literary figures. Remains of small landscape garden with pond and summer house; eye-catcher on distant ridge.

Manygates, Barnsley Road, Wakefield: brick house of two storeys with further attic storey. Entrance via Tuscan order portico raised above semi-basement on landing supported on Greek Doric columns. Built 1849-50 for Edward Green snr, ironfounder.

Meanwood Towers, Meanwood, Leeds: profusely detailed Gothic house built for Leeds engineer Thomas Stuart Kennedy, to designs of E.W. Pugin *c.* 1867. Tower redesigned by R.N. Shaw. Glastonbury-style kitchen survives. Now badly mutilated.

Meltham Hall, Meltham Mills: Greek Revival villa with vigorous acanthus ornamentation, built *c.* 1841 for William Leigh Brook, cotton thread manufacturer. Later extensions. Stands in public park with access to grounds.

Menston Hall, Menston: gentry house with central range of *c.* 1740 in Classical style showing vernacular influence. Acquired by James Padgett, woollen manufacturer and dyer, in 1876 and extended *c.* 1876-78 with large Italianate wings and tower (latter demolished) to create residence in palazzo style. Private homes still, but stands in public park.

Millbank Hall, or Milner Lodge, Luddendenfoot: small, but beautifully detailed house probably built for William Currer of Boyes Mill who died in 1807 when the house was described as 'newly built' [I am grateful to David Cant for this information]. Best front of ashlar with tripartite windows beneath relieving arches; Greek Doric portico to entrance front with half flutes to columns. Parapet conceals chimneys. Interior has remains of fine neo-classical detailing, also early bathroom with marble bath. Builder unknown, but occupied by Jonathan Akroyd, worsted spinner; architect unknown. Now derelict.

Moorfield House, Headingley, Leeds: richly detailed Gothic house with octagonal tower, castellations and Elizabethan porch. Dates probably from mid-1860s (is roof to bay window later?) and was built for the chemical manufacturer William Glover Joy.

Moorville, Burley-in-Wharfedale: Scottish Baronial-style house built 1848 for J.H. Whitehead of Leeds, stuff dyer, and possibly enlarged by Hudson family, textile magnates, who occupied house much of nineteenth century. Originally a large and impressive house with two towers, but now only a part survives.

Northgate Mount, Honley: neo-classical villa with central canted bay window built *c.* 1825 for William Brooke, woollen manufacturer.

Oakbank, Ingrow, Keighley: Italianate house in Classical style built of ashlar with heavy bracketed canopy to entrance. Villa planning with impressive central hall and staircase, arcaded with much Italianate detailing. Built for John Haggas, worsted spinner and manufacturer in 1872. Lockwood & Mawson?

Oaklands, Dalton: undistinguished, but pleasant Gothic house built for Robert Henry Tolson, fancy manufacturer, *c.* 1855. Tower-like entrance porch with oriel. Public footpath leads through former garden and past house.

Oak Lea, Long Causeway, Adel: superb Elizbethan-style house with curvilinear gables and oriel. Built 1871-77? for dye-stuff manufacturer William Croysdale.

Oakwood, Bingley: French influence Gothic house of 1864/5 by Knowles & Wilcock for Thomas Garnett, wool merchant. Interiors by Burges and glass by Morris. Severely mutilated in 1960s when much of Burges's work was destroyed.

Oakwood, Roundhay, Leeds: Classical house of early nineteenth century with storeyed bay windows; probably designed for wool merchant Robert Hudson.

Oatsroyd House, Luddenden: seventeenth-century house with new front in Classical Italianate style added mid-nineteenth century. Stands adjacent to Oatsroyd Mill and home of Murgatroyd family, worsted spinners and manufacturers. Architects of new work possibly Dearden family.

Park House, Queensbury: house built in 1890s probably for R. Lionel Foster. Arts and Crafts-influenced Manor House style with tall chimneys and storeyed bay windows, somewhat like the work of Bradford architect Ellis Marten.

Pierremont, Bradford: basically small villa of 1860s, but enlarged by the worsted manufacturer Fredrick Priestman over a number of years. Partly demolished, but enough remains to show that interior remodelled *c.* 1880-1900 in accomplished Queen Anne style, with superb quality Arts and Crafts painted and stained glass in hall and staircase windows. Some earlier work survives. Largely Milnes & France.

Potter Newton Mansion – see Harehills Grove.

Prospect House, Queensbury: small rubble-built house of *c.* 1827 with later extensions for John Foster snr of Black Dyke Mills, worsted manufacturer. Exceedingly modest house – considering Foster's wealth – of vernacular quality.

Ravensknowle, Huddersfield: palazzo-style house built for John Beaumont, textile designer and manufacturer, by Richard Tress 1850s to '60s. Impressive Classical detail with first-floor loggia above main entrance. Museum – public access to house and grounds.

Rein Wood, Marsh, Huddersfield: Italianate house of mid-nineteenth century origins, but extended over the years, notably in 1900 by John Kirk & Sons for the stockbroker F.W. Bentley. Remains of extensive water garden.

Rock House, Horbury: large Elizabethan-style house, well articulated with curvilinear gables, and set on high ground above Horbury. Built for George Harrop, woollen manufacturer, between 1873 and 1877.

Royds Wood, Cliffe End, Huddersfield: house of *c*. 1868 for Sir Joseph Crosland, banking and textiles. Original house showed French Classical influences. Now only a scrap of it remains, incorporated into a school built early this century.

St Anne's Tower, Headingley, Leeds: Elizabethan-style house built in 1860 for T.R. Harding hackle pin and comb manufacturer. Castellated entrance porch with oriel, falling roofline to service range and further tower.

Sandal Grange, Sandal Magna, Wakefield: Gothic house built originally by Laurence Hitchon, a Wakefield woolstapler, in 1840s; acquired by worsted spinner T.W. Marriott in 1867 and enlarged. Result: bland, but pleasant Gothic house with entrance tower.

Shipley Fields Hall, Hilton Drive, Shipley: rebuilding of seventeenth- or eighteenth-century house probably in 1830s by worsted manufacturer Joseph Hargreaves. Small villa with Greek-derived detail to front and older vernacular detail to rear. Good surviving exterior wash house/laundry. Divided into two houses in 1907 when interior was remodelled.

Spenfield, Headingley, Leeds: villa built *c*. 1877 for the banker James Walker Oxley. Designed by George Corson in uneasy combination of gables, bay windows and French roofs; extended later nineteenth century with addition of billiard room. Remarkable for its Aesthetic Movement interior by G.F. Armitage.

Springfield, North St, Keighley: late neo-classical villa built for the machine maker R.L. Hattersley, probably in the 1860s. Urban site on main road with little garden; an unusually modest villa given Hattersley's wealth, but finely detailed.

Spring Hall, Spring Hall Lane, Halifax: rebuilding of earlier house in 1870-1871 for the worsted manufacturer Thomas Holdsworth; W.S. Barber, architect [I am grateful to Tony Heginbottom for this information]. Pennine Manor House in style, but with the unusual addition of octagonal tower. House extended in 1887 with billiard room and probably some further remodelling

Steeton Manor, Steeton: tall Pennine Manor House design set on side of Aire Valley and built in local stone with stone roof. Impressive porch to rear and originally formal garden. Built 1895 by Sir Swire Smith, worsted spinner, to designs of W.H. Sugden.

Stansfield Hall, near Todmorden: enlargement of earlier vernacular house for Joshua Fielden by John Gibson. Convincing early Tudor style that sits well with the old house, and most unlike Gibson's Dobroyd Castle, qv; built for Joshua's brother John jnr.

Stoneleigh, Bryan Road, Huddersfield: large Gothic house in mixed English styles built on suburban site around 1860-65 for Edward Beaumont, cigar manufacturer. Impressive arcaded porch. Remains of water garden.

Upper Shibden Hall, Catherine Slack, Northowram: small neo-classical house with central storeyed bay window and added – though near contemporary – tower. Built for Michael Stocks, colliery owner and brewer; 1800-20? Now in ruinous condition and in danger of collapse.

Weetwood Croft, Weetwood, Leeds: Arts and Crafts house in Manor House style designed in 1896 (despite external date 1898) by Francis W. Bedford for George William Brown, worsted merchant possibly as a part of the development of his Weetwood estate. Retains original hall with inglenook, delft tiles and, unusually, mahogany panelling.

Weetwood Lodge, Weetwood, Leeds: French-style villa with sweeping roof to entrance tower, lucarns, false machicolations, tracery head to main entrance. Built around 1870-1875 for the newspaper magnate Frederick Baines.

Weetwood Villa, Weetwood, Leeds: originally superb Elizabethan house of around 1861-67, built for the banker Henry Oxley. Elizabethan tower to garden entrance on terrace, but with (later?) French roof; this entrance turned into bay window perhaps end of century.

Wharfeside, Burley-in-Wharfedale: built *c.* 1851 for the worsted spinner and MP W.E. Forster. Gabled elevation, bay windows with French roofs and tower with mitre roof terminating main block.

Wheatfield, Wood Lane, Headingley, Leeds: pleasant house in rural Italianate style with tower to entrance porch. Perhaps built in mid-1860s for Isaac Israel, a woollen merchant, but later occupied by Joseph Nicholson chemical manufacturer. Extended towards end of century and stables rebuilt in powerful baroque style.

Whinburn, Hollins Lane, Keighley: important house built for the textile machine maker Prince Smith III, later Sir Prince Prince-Smith. First build 1897 by James Ledingham in tall Manor House style; enlarged 1912/13 to designs of Simpson & Ayrton with baronial hall and looks of fortified house. Superb craftsmanship preserved throughout interior. Gardens probably by Thomas H. Mawson *c.* 1913 – canal, summer house, belvedere, remains of pergola.

Whiteshaw, Long Causeway, Denholme: gradual replacement of earlier house by Foster family, worsted manufacturers of Denholme Mills. First, small neo-classical house of 1840-60?, John Dearden? Additions to eastern gable 1870, Milnes & France; additions to western gable 1884, Milnes & France. Result was long Italianate house. Garden terrace and remains of croquet lawn and original bedding.

Willow Bank, Edgerton, Huddersfield: Gothic house built for the wool merchant Thomas Hirst in 1850s. Hall range and crosswing with octagonal tower; castellated outbuildings. Set on bank high above the road in suburban setting.

Wilshaw Villa, Wilshaw: small house in vernacular style built *c.* 1832 for Joseph Hirst, fancy and woollen cloth manufacturer.

Woodlands, Wilton Park, Upper Batley: plain, but handsome Gothic villa built for the woollen manufacturer George Sheard between 1873 and 1875 to the designs of Sheard

& Hanstock. Pointed arch windows, French spire to entrance, now unfortunately re-roofed with copper instead of original Westmorland slates hung in contrasting patterns. A little of the interior decoration of the drawing room survives. Museum – public access to house and grounds.

Woodlands, Gelderd Road, Gildersome: house built *c.* 1880 to designs of Sheard & Hanstock for woollen manufacturer George Webster. Competent Queen Anne style with Dutch gables and good-quality relief carving in applied panels. Enlarged *c.* 1900, probably for Wilson family, woollen manufacturers, to make two dwellings, but so skilfully done that new work indistinguishable from old.

Woodlands, West Avenue, Roundhay: rebuilding of previous house in hard French baroque style. Small Tuscan portico to entrance front with heavy central accenting, bay windows, pedimented lucarnes. Long service wing with sundial to east; stable yard with clock to rear. Later extension (billiard room?) mars design. Built for woollen manufacturer William Jagger Cooper in 1879.

Woodleigh Hall, Cragg Wood, Rawden: large Elizabethan-style house with renaissance overtones built *c.* 1869 for the worsted manufacturer Moses Bottomley to a design by Lockwood & Mawson. Loggia and conservatory of contemporary date survive. House stands on a terrace overlooking remains of garden that blends with surrounding trees and landscape.

Woodsley House, Clarendon Road, Leeds: compact late neo-classical house built of brick with stone dressings. Expensively Classical interior with remains of Pompeian decoration to (?) dining room. Built 1840/1 for Sir Peter Fairbairn, machine maker, and thought to be by John Clark. Queen Victoria really did sleep here on her visit to Leeds in 1858.

END NOTES

Introduction

1 Smith, William, *Morley: Ancient and Modern*, London, 1886.
2 Rubinstein, W.D., *Men of Property: The Very Wealthy in Britain Since the Industrial Revolution*, London, 1981.
3 Reynolds, Jack, *The Great Paternalist: Titus Salt and the Growth of Nineteenth-Century Bradford'*, London, 1983.
4 Foster, J., *Class Struggle and the Industrial Revolution*, London, 1974.
5 Rubinstein, W.D., *Men of Property*, London, 1981.
6 Linstrum, Derek, *West Yorkshire Architects and Architecture*, London, 1978.

Chapter 1

1 Details from the Earl of Harewood's Archive, WYAS, Leeds; also discussed in Kennedy, C., *Harewood: The Life and Times of an English Country House*, London, 1982.
2 All of these figures were taken from Bateman, L., *The Great Landowners of Great Britain and Ireland*, London, 1879.
3 The figures that Behrens was interested in were collated and analysed in Cudworth, William, *Condition of the Industrial Classes of Bradford and District*, Bradford, 1885.
4 For example, Davidoff, L. and Hall, C., *Family Fortunes: Men and Women of the English Middle Class 1780-1850*, London, 1987.
5 PP vol. XXXIX pt II 'A Return Showing the Number of Persons Charged Income Tax for the years ending 5th April 1858 and 1859'.
6 Reynolds, Jack, *The Great Paternalist: Titus Salt and the Growth of Nineteenth-Century Bradford* – on p. 65, 1871 seems to be a misprint for 1880.
7 Rubinstein, W.D., *Men of Property*, London, 1981.
8 See, for example, PP 1882 vol. LII, 'Return Relating to Parliamentary Constituencies (Population etc.)'.
9 PP 1861 vol. XVII, 'Twenty-Second Annual Report of the Registrar General of Births, Marriages and Deaths'.
10 Cudworth, William, *Round About Bradford*, Bradford, 1876.
11 Messrs Rennie, Broun, Shirref, *General View of the Agriculture of the West Riding*, London, 1794.
12 For Marshall see Rimmer, W.G., *Marshalls of Leeds Flax Spinners 1788-1886*, Cambridge, 1960; for Gott see Hudson, Pat, *The Genesis of Industrial Capital*, Cambridge, 1986.

13 I am grateful to Colum Giles and Ian Goodhal of the former RCHME, now English Heritage.

14 Smiles, Samuel, *Self Help*, London, 1859.

15 Mayhall, J., *Annals of Leeds, York and the Surrounding Districts*, Leeds, 1860.

16 Taylor, T.C., *One Hundred Years*, Leeds, 1946.

17 For a history of the Shaw family see, Shaw, R.M., *The Shaws of Stainland*, The Transactions of the Halifax Antiquarian Society, 1965.

18 Sigsworth, Eric, *Black Dyke Mills*, Liverpool, 1958.

19 For a discussion of this point in a national context see Crouzet, F., *The First Industrialists: the Problem of Origins*, Cambridge, 1985.

20 Rubinstein, W.D., *British Millionaires 1809-1949*, Bulletin of the Institute of Historical Research, vol. XLVII, 1974.

21 Payne, B., Payne, D., 'Extracts from the Journals of John Deakin Heaton MD', Thoresby Society Publication 53 ; Miscellany 15, pt II, 1972.

22 For further discussion of this point see Wolff, J., Seed, J., *The Culture of Capital*, Manchester, 1988.

Chapter 2

1 Roundhay Park, Leeds, would make a third, but has not been included, since its builders, the Nicholsons, do not match the selection criteria outlined in the introduction; Greenholme Villa, Burley-in-Wharfedale, may have been a fourth, but it has been demolished virtually without record.

2 See, for example, Linstrum, Derek, *West Yorkshire Architects and Architecture*, London, 1978.

3 Greenwood's Map of Yorkshire, for example.

4 I am grateful to Mr David Cant for this information.

5 BCL, BUN 1852 PLA.

6 Parker, J.H., *A Concise Glossary of Terms*, Oxford, 1846.

7 Parker, J.H., *An Introduction to the Study of Gothic Architecture*, Oxford, 1849.

8 Loudon, J.C., *An Encyclopaedia of Cottage, Farm, and Villa Architecture*, London, 1833.

9 Plans amongst the papers relating to Black Dyke Mills have now been deposited at WYAS, Bradford.

10 BCL 'Milner Field For Sale'.

11 Linstrum 'West Yorkshire Architects'.

12 Girouard, Mark, *The Victorian Country House*, Oxford, 1971.

13 Property of the owner.

14 RCHME Yorkshire Textile Mills Survey: Oats Royd Mills file, NBR No. 62704.

15 Airville, Shipley, is a good example of his work on smaller villas.

16 Halifax Council Building Plan 354 (I am grateful to Tony Heginbottam for this information).

17 This and the following quotations are from Muthesius, Herman, *The English House*, New York, 1987 (original 1904).

18 Muthesius, *English House*.

19 *The British Architect,* 1895, vol. 44, p. 291 passim.

Chapter 3

1 Kerr, Robert, *The Gentleman's House*, London, 1864.

2 For a detailed chronology of this house see Franklin, Gill, *Edwardian Butterfly Houses* in *Architectural Review* vol. CLVII, No. 938, April 1975.

3 Kerr, *Gentleman's House*; all further quotations mentioning Kerr are from this source.

4 Quoted in Franklin, Gill, *The Gentleman's Country House and its Pplan, 1835-1914*, London, 1981.

5 Beeton, Isabella, *Beeton's Book of Household Management*, London, 1861.

6 Muthesius, Herman, *The English House*, New York, 1987 (1904).

7 Kerr, *Gentleman's House*.

8 *Ibid*

9 Mathewman, J., *Masonic Addresses of Thomas Tew J.P.*, London, 1892.

10 Balgarnie, Revd R., *Sir Titus Salt, Baronet, His Life and its Lessons*, London, 1887.

11 Quoted in Reid, W.T., *The Life of the Right Honourable Willam Edward Forster*, London, 1888.

12 Percy, C. & Ridley, J., *The Letters of Sir Edwin Lutyens to his Wife Lady Emily*, London, 1985.

13 Giroaurd, Mark, *The Victorian Country House*, Oxford, 1971; *Life in the English Country House*, Yale, 1978; Franklin, *Gentleman's Country House*.

14 Sale catalogue BCL.

15 Hopwood, W.A. & Casperson, F., *Meanwood*, Leeds, 1986.

16 Constantine, J., *Sir Isaac Holden, Bart., and his Theory of Healthy Long Life*, Manchester, 1898.

17 Franklin, Gill, *Troops of Servants: labour and planning in the country house 1840-1914*, Victorian Studies, vol. XIX, no. 2, 1975.

18 Given the ninety-two families selected for this study and the larger number of households they created, eighty-two may seem small. However, using the Census has its limits. A number of heads of households had died before 1841, while some had set up house only after 1891. Other families were absent on Census night, and, thus, the details provided could be misleading. The 1841 Census was used as little as possible, because it rarely gives full information about servants – they might be recorded simply as 'female servant', rather than, say, 'scullery maid'. A minority of families simply could not be located. A further danger is that the Census does not allow for servants' nights off, nor those living outside the house. The figures quoted above, therefore, have to be taken on the basis of the best information available.

19 Kerr, *Gentleman's House*.

20 Percy & Ridley, *Letters of Sir Edwin Lutyens*.

21 Kerr, *Gentleman's House*.

22 Brotherton Library, Special Collections, University of Leeds – John Foster & Sons: Personal Letters of John Foster/240 23rd January, 1862.

23 Quoted in Hardman, Malcolm, *Ruskin and Bradford*, Manchester, 1986.

24 Healey, E., *A Series of Picturesque Views of Castles and Country Houses in Yorkshire*, Bradford, 1885.

25 Healey, *Picturesque Views* and all other quotations in this paragraph.

26 All Healey, *Picturesque Views*.

27 Illingworth, E.H., *The Holden-Illingworth Letters*, Bradford, 1927.

28 Constantine, *Sir Isaac Holden, Bart*.

Chapter 4

1 This is now in the Paul Mellon Collection at Yale University. For a fuller discussion of Repton's work at Armley see Sheeran, George, *Landscape Gardens in West Yorkshire 1680-1880*, Wakefield, 1990. All further quotations about Armley are from the Red Book.

2 Healey, *Picturesque Views*.

3 Healey, *Picturesque Views*.

4 See Elliott, Brent, *Victorian Gardens*, London, 1986.

5 Hibberd, Shirley, *Rustic Adornments for Homes of Taste*, London, 1856.

6 Major, J., *The Theory and Practice of Landscape Gardening*, London, 1852.

7 The plan is at Cliffe Castle Museum, Keighley.

8 Kerr, R., *The Gentleman's House*, London, 1864; and all other quotations in this section marked Kerr.

9 For a wide-ranging discussion of conservatories and other glasshouses see Woods, M. & Warren, A., *Glass Houses*, London, 1988.

10 Healey, *Picturesque Views.*

11 Kerr, *Gentleman's House.*

12 Quoted in Franklin, Gill, *The Gentleman's Country House and its Plan, 1835-1914*, London, 1981.

13 Balgarnie, Revd R., *Sir Titus Salt, Baronet, His Life and its Lessons*, London, 1887.

14 Balgarnie, *Sir Titus Salt.*

15 *Gardener's Chronicle,* 13 May 1871.

Chapter 5

1 City of Bradford Metropolitan District Council Libraries Division, *The Journal of Dr John Simpson of Bradford 1825*, Bradford, 1981.

2 Quoted in Daniels, Stephen, 'Landscaping for a Manufacturer' in *Journal of Historical Geography*, 1981.

3 Healey, E., *A Series of Picturesque Views of Castles and Country Houses in Yorkshire*, Bradford, 1885.

4 Illingworth, E.H., *The Holden-Illingworth Letters*, Bradford, 1927.

5 Illingworth, *Holden Letters.*

6 Obituary, *Yorkshire Observer*, 10 October 1924.

7 Quoted in Illingworth, T., *Yeadon, Yorkshire*, Yeadon, 1980.

8 Sigsworth, Eric, *Black Dyke Mills*, Liverpool, 1958.

9 For an account of the Greens see the National Trust Guide Book to the Treasurer's House, from which this quotation is taken. Also Raper, E.L., *A Green Background*, Wakefield, 1977, a hard-to-find limited edition of thirty-five copies, but one is at Wakefield Library.

10 As above.

11 For Kitson see Kitson-Clark Papers at WYAS, Leeds, and Morris, R.J., *The Rise of James Kitson*, Thoresby Society Publications, Miscellany, 15, part 3, 1973; for Dearman Birchall see Verey, D., *The Diary of a Victorian Squire*, Gloucester, 1983.

12 Rubinstein, W.D., *Men of Property*, London, 1981; Trainor, R.H., *Black Country Elites: the Exercise of Authority in an Industrialized Area 1830-1900*, Oxford, 1993; Smeets, Elyze, 'New Money and the Land Market: Landownership in 19th-Century Twente, the Netherlands' in Palang, H. *et al* (eds), *European Rural Landscapes: Persistence and Change in a Globalising Environment*, Kluwer Academic Publishers, 2004.

13 Girouard, Mark, *Life in the English Country House*, Yale, 1978.

14 Cliffe Castle Museum, Butterfield Letters, Box 1, Packet D, 7 July 1878.

15 Fox, W.J., *Morality and the Classes of Society*, London, 1835.

16 For a discussion of this point see Church, R.A., *The Great Victorian Boom, 1850-1873*, London, 1975.

17 The graph, of course, relates only to the houses selected for this study. In one respect it is in need of revision: it does not take account of the families or younger generations of families who were beginning to make their mark in the period 1890-1914, and enjoyed their greatest period of financial success after that date. Several of these families were building good houses at the beginning of the twentieth century. If the graph were to reflect the house-building pattern more accurately, then it should show a small rise, rather than a decline, between 1890 and 1914.

18 Balgarnie, Revd R., *Sir Titus Salt, Baronet, His Life and its Lessons*, London, 1887.

Ten Case Studies

1 Brotherton Library, University of Leeds, Gott Papers, Section II, 194/2/53. This a series of accounts and estimates mostly for the rebuilding of Armley House. Estimates were taken and contracts signed with various tradesmen in 1816; the masons' bills were settled in May and August 1817; the last tradesmen's bill, the painters', was settled in October

1817. Smirke's design for the house has previously been an attribution only. These accounts confirm he was the architect – e.g. 194/2/53/51 which is headed 'An estimate of Carpenters and Joiners work Specified as under, agreeable to Mr Smirks Plan for the alterations of Armley House belonging to B. Gott Esq.' dated 9th ? 1816.

2 It has been suggested (see Lovell 1986) that Smirke modelled the house on the Temple of Hephaestus in Athens, because of the way the bay window projects into the colonnade, and also because one of Gott's sons died in September 1817, while touring Greece and was buried in the same temple. However, since the Hephaisteion is a Doric Temple and Armley House uses the Ionic order, since the projection into the colonnade at the temple is later medieval work not worthy of copying, and since the bay window at Armley House pre-dates Smirke's alterations which were drawn up and completed before Gott's son died, this seems unlikely.

3 Quoted in Linstrum, Derek, *West Yorkshire Architects and Architecture*, London, 1978.

4 Plans at WYAS Bradford, Deposited Building Plans 197 and 3547.

5 Quoted in Hanson, T.W., *The Story of Old Halifax*, Halifax, 1920.

6 Elevation at WYAS Calderdale, MISC: 713.

7 I should like to thank Nigel Herring, Keeper of Art at the Bankfield Museum, for sharing his knowledge of the house with me.

8 *The British Architect*, 1874, vol. 2, pp 377–8.

9 WYAS Leeds, Sale Plans, Hepper 767.

10 I am grateful to Mr Gorden Burton of Wakefield MDC for finding the original plans for me among the many hundreds of nineteenth-century plans that the council still holds.

11 Both Ledingham's and Simpson & Ayrton's plans are amongst the deposited building plans at Keighley Reference Library.

12 See Linstrum, *West Yorkshire Architects and Architecture*, or Gradidge, R., *Dream Houses: The Edwardian Ideal*, London, 1980.

13 This assumes that Lutyens knew of these houses. Contemporaries (e.g. *Country Life*, 1910) thought the house Palladian in style, and Lutyens himself made allusions to Palladio, although he also suggested that he had been influenced by the Italian renaissance architect Michele Sanmicheli, but it is difficult to see how or by what.

BIBLIOGRAPHY

Almond, A., *Biography of James Ickringill*, Keighley, 1919

Balgarnie, R., *Sir Titus Salt, Baronet*, London, 1877
Bateman, L., *The Great Landowners of Great Britain and Ireland*, London, 1879
Beaumont, W.W., *Motor Vehicles and Motors*, London, 1900
Beeton, I., *Beeton's Book of Household Management*, London, 1861

Chapman, S.D., *The Early Factory Masters*, Newton Abbot, 1967
Church, R.A., *The Great Victorian Boom, 1850-1873*, London, 1975
Constantine, J., *Sir Isaac Holden, Bart., and his Theory of Healthy Long Life*, Manchester, 1898
Crouzet, F., *The First Industrialists, The Problems of Origins*, Cambridge, 1985
Crump, W.B. and Ghorbal, G., *History of the Huddersfield Woollen Industry*, Huddersfield, 1935
Cudworth, W., *Condition of the Industrial Classes of Bradford and District*, Bradford, 1885
Ibid., *The Histories of Bolton and Bowling*, Bradford, 1891

Daniels, S., 'Landscaping for a Manufacturer', *Journal of Historical Geography*, 1981
Davidoff, L. and Hall, C., "*Family Fortunes: Men and Women of the English Middle Class, 1780-1850*, London, 1987

Elliott, B., *Victorian Gardens*, London, 1986

Foster, J., *Class Struggle and the Industrial Revolution*, London, 1974
Fox, W.J., *Morality and the Classes of Society*, London, 1835
Franklin, J., 'Edwardian Butterfly Houses', *Architectural Review*, vol. CLVII, no. 938, April, 1975a
Ibid., 'Troops of Servants: labour and planning in the country house 1840-1914', *Victorian Studies*, vol. XIX, no. 2, 1975b
Ibid., 'The Gentleman's Country House and Its Plan, 1835-1914', London, 1981

Girouard, M., *The Victorian Country House*, Oxford, 1971
Ibid., *Life in the English Country House*, Yale, 1978
Gradidge, R., *Dream Houses: the Edwardian Ideal*, London, 1980
Ibid., *Edwin Lutyens, architect laureate*, London, 1981
Grainge, W., *The History and Topography of Harrogate and the Forest of Knaresborough*, London, 1871

Hardman, M., *Ruskin and Bradford*, Manchester, 1986

Healey, E., *A Series of Picturesque Views of Castles and Country Houses in Yorkshire*, Bradford, 1885

Honeyman, K., *Origins of Enterprise, Business Leadership in the Industrial Revolution*, Manchester, 1982

Hopwood, W.A., and Casperson F.P., *Meanwood*, Leeds, 1986

Howe, A., *The Cotton Masters, 1830-1860*, Oxford, 1984

Hudson, P., *The Genesis of Industrial Capital*, Cambridge, 1986

Hussey, C., *The Life of Sir Edwin Lutyens*, London, 1950

Illingworth, E.H., *The Holden-Illingworth Letters*, Bradford, 1927

Illingworth, T., *Yeadon, Yorkshire*, Yeadon, 1980

Johnson, K.I., *The Armley Schulze Organ*, Leeds, 1985

Kennedy, C., *Harewood The Life and Times of an English Country House*, London, 1982

Kerr, R., *The Gentleman's House*, London, 1864

Lackey, C., *Quality Pays: the Story of Joshua Tetley and Son*, Ascot, 1985

Loudon, J.C., *An Encyclopaedia of Cottage, Farm and Villa Architecture*, London, 1833

Lovell, V., 'Benjamin Gott of Armley House, Leeds, 1762-1840: Patron of the Arts', Thoresby Society Publications, vol. 18, part 2, 1986

Major, J., *The Theory and Practice of Landscape Gardening*, London, 1852

Mathewman, J., *Masonic Addresses of Thomas Tew JP*, London, 1892

Mayhall, J., *Annals of Leeds, York, and the Surrounding Districts*, Leeds, 1860

Morris, R.J., 'The Rise of James Kitson', Thoresby Society Publications Miscellany 15, part 3, 1973

Ibid., "Class, sect and party The making of the British middle class, Leeds 1820-1850", Manchester, 1990

Muthesius, H., *The English House* (Translation by Janet Seligman of original Berlin edition of 1904/5) New York, 1987

Muthesius, S., *The High Victorian Movement in Architecture*, London, 1972

Payne, B. and D., 'Extracts from the Journals of John Deakin Heaton, MD', Thoresby Society Publication 53; Miscellany 15, part II, 1972

Payne, P.L., *British Entrepreneurship in the 19th Century*, London, 1988

Parker, J., *Illustrated Rambles from Hipperolme to Tong*, Bradford, 1904

Parker, J.H., *A Concise Glossary of Terms*, Oxford, 1846

Ibid., *An Introduction to the Study of Gothic Architecture*, Oxford, 1849

Percy, C. and Ridley, J., *The Letters of Sir Edwin Lutyens to his Wife Lady Emily*, London, 1985

Raper, E.L., *A Green Background*, Wakefield, 1977

Reid, W.T., *Life of the Right Honorable William Edward Forster*, London, 1888

Rennie, Broun, Shirref, *General View of the Agriculture of the West Riding*, London, 1794

Reynolds, J., *The Great Paternalist Titus Salt and the Growth of Nineteenth-Century Bradford*, London, 1983

Rimmer, W.G., *Marshalls of Leeds, Flax Spinners 1788-1886*, Cambridge, 1960

Rubinstein, W.D., 'British Millionaires 1809-1949', Bulletin of the Institute of Historical Research, vol. XLVII, 1974

Ibid., 'The Victorian Middle Classes: Wealth Occupation and Geography', *Economic History Review*, 2nd series, vol. 30, 1977

Ibid., *Men of Property*, London, 1981

Scott, W.H. and Pike, W.T. (Eds), *The West Riding of Yorkshire at the Opening of the Twentieth Century. Contemporary Biographies*, Brighton, 1902

Shaw, R.M., *The Shaws of Stainland*, Transactions Halifax Antiquarian Society, 1965

Sheeran, G., *Landscape Gardens in West Yorkshire 1680-1880*, Wakefield, 1990

Smeets, E., 'New Money and the Land Market: Landownership in 19th-Century Twente, the Netherlands' (in Palang, H. *et al* (eds), *European Rural Landscapes: Persistence and Change in a Globalising Environment*, Kluwer Academic Publishers, 2004)

Smith, W., *Morley: Ancient and Modern*, London, 1886

Snowden, K., *The Master Spinner*, London, 1922

Taylor, R.V., *The Biographia Leodiensis*, London, 1865

Taylor, R.V., *Supplement to the Biographia Leodiensis*, London, 1867

Trainor, R.H., *Black Country Elites: the Exercise of Authority in an Industrialized Area 1830-1900*, Oxford, 1993

Verey, D., *The Diary of a Victorian Squire*, Gloucester, 1983

Wolff, J., and Seed, J., *The Culture of Capital*, Manchester, 1988

Woods, M., and Warren, A., *Glass Houses*, London, 1988

INDEX

Page numbers in **bold** refer to illustrations.

'A well-illustrated, scholarly, but readable account' – *Telegraph & Argus*

The West Yorkshire families who grew rich through commerce and industry during the Industrial Revolution used their newly acquired wealth to build houses and gardens that were markedly different from those of older landed and commercial families. *Brass Castles* is the first book to explore these nineteenth-century mansions as a group in their own right.

In this fascinating sociological approach to architectural history, George Sheeran examines the urban as well as the rural homes of ninety-two of the wealthiest families from the 'New Rich' section of the population. He analyses their wealth and where it came from, contrasts the architecture and functions of their houses, compares them with the general development of the nineteenth-century house and looks at how far they were modified by local or individual conditions.

George Sheeran is Head of the Pennine and Yorkshire Studies Unit at the University of Bradford where he teaches and researches urban, architectural and landscape history.

ISBN 0-7524-3806-9

9 780752 438061

www.tempus-publishing.com

£14.99

Tempus Publishing Ltd
The Mill, Brimscombe Port,
Stroud, Gloucestershire
GL5 2QG UK

Front cover: West Royd, Farsley, designed by Andrews & Pepper for John O. Butler in 1866.

Back cover: Ravensknowle, Huddersfield, designed by Richard Tress for John Beaumont *c.* 1859.